THE COMING KING

THE COMING KING

Compiled and edited by
Gerald B. Smith

STL Books
Bromley, Kent

Kingsway Publications
Eastbourne

Copyright © 1989 Christian Publications

First published in the USA as *Jesus Is Victor*
by Christian Publications, 3825 Hartzdale Drive,
Camp Hill, PA 17011

First British (Anglicised) edition 1990

Biblical quotations are from the New International Version of the
Holy Bible, copyright © 1973, 1978, 1984 by International Bible
Society. Used by permission of Hodder and Stoughton Ltd.

British Library Cataloguing in Publication Data

Tozer, A. W. (Aiden Wilson) *1897–1963*
  The Coming King.
  1. Bible. N. T. Revelation
  I. Title II. Smith, Gerald
  228

  ISBN 1–85078–074–9

STL Books are published in England by Send The Light
(Operation Mobilisation), PO Box 48, Bromley, Kent, BR1 3JH

Published in co-operation with Kingsway Publications Ltd,
1 St Anne's Road, Eastbourne, E. Sussex, BN21 3UN

Production and Printing in England by
Nuprint Ltd, 30b Station Road, Harpenden, Herts, AL5 4SE

Contents

Editor's Introduction

Aiden Wilson Tozer is remembered by many as an effective preacher of God's written word. And those who knew him best testify to his consistent practice of the truths he proclaimed. In the years since his death in 1963, there has been among conservative Christianity a growing wave of respect and gratitude for this Spirit-taught 'prophet' of our century.

When, upon his death, it was discovered that Tozer had left no unpublished book manuscripts, the editors at Christian Publications turned to the depository of his weekly sermons, electronically recorded both in Chicago and Toronto. From those sermons have come many of the posthumous books bearing his name.

This volume is the last from that source. In Toronto in 1961, Tozer preached a series of messages from the book of Revelation. Unfortunately only fourteen tapes, covering the first ten chapters, can be located. That explains why this volume of twelve chapters cannot be considered an exposition of the entire book. Rather, it should be received as a volume of still timely spiritual lessons discovered and preached by Tozer in the mature years of his long public ministry.

Surely it would have been the author's desire that all who pursue the truth in Revelation determine to be among the 'overcomers'—resting their faith alone on the goodness and grace of a loving and just Creator God.

Gerald B. Smith
Fort Myers, Florida, USA
1989

Preface

The following paragraphs are the thoughts and words of the author, A.W. Tozer, as he explained to his Toronto congregation his own approach to the Revelation.

The Revelation is a great book because it is the Revelation of Jesus Christ! It is not, as some suppose, a book just for theologians, scholars and historians. Although the book presents a complex message, it was written for ordinary people like us.

We have choices as to what we will do with it. I warn you that it is entirely possible to turn this book into a source of blight to your soul. On the other hand, it is possible to find in it a great source of light and blessing.

As far as I am concerned, we are dealing here with the word of God. To try to plumb divine mysteries and to learn divine truth without sorrow in our hearts and tears in our eyes is vanity and futility ten times multiplied.

Revelation raises questions that none of us can answer. There are many details in God's plan for the end of this age that we do not know. Admittedly, some preachers seem able to preach wonderful sermons about things they do not know, but I refuse to be placed in that category.

Here is the method that I must follow as we proceed in our study:

* I will not attempt to interpret or explain all of the symbols and figures of speech as they appear.
* I will not arbitrarily force every passage to fit some prophetic pattern or idea. (If you want to take that route—which, I repeat, I will not take—I warn you that you may do it at the terrible expense of spiritual dishonesty! Or, short of that, you will narrow down your mind to a point where you can never expand or grow—where the Lord can find nothing further to say to you.)
* I will freely admit that there are symbols, personalities and figures that I cannot understand or explain.
* Positively, I will identify the main points to discover the underlying spiritual lessons.
* I will emphasise the great central truth that dominates the Revelation: the truth that when God in heaven gets enough of this world's sin and rejection, violence and rebellion, He will wait no longer. He will do something about it!

We need not decipher and decode mysterious symbols to determine the outcome of this conflict of the ages. There is a plain and radiant theme from the beginning to the end of the Revelation: Jesus is victor!

That theme will be our theme in these meditations.

A.W. Tozer
Toronto
1961

1

The Theme—Jesus Is Victor

*The revelation of Jesus Christ, which God gave him
to show his servants what must soon take place. He
made it known by sending his angel to his servant
John, who testifies to everything he saw—that is, the
word of God and the testimony of Jesus Christ.
Blessed is the one who reads the words of this
prophecy, and blessed are those who hear it and
take to heart what is written in it, because the time is
near....*

*I warn everyone who hears the words of the
prophecy of this book: If anyone adds anything to
them, God will add to him the plagues described in
this book. And if anyone takes words away from
this book of prophecy, God will take away from
him his share in the tree of life and in the holy city,
which are described in this book.*

*He who testifies to these things says, 'Yes, I am
coming soon.'*

Amen. Come, Lord Jesus.

*The grace of the Lord Jesus be with God's
people. Amen.*

Revelation 1:1–3; 22:18–21

Have you ever heard of a person eagerly reading an interesting book, then suddenly deciding to abandon it without reading the last chapter? The last chapter ties together the threads of the narrative; it summarises the arguments; it climaxes the action. You and I would agree that to close a book without reading the final chapter would be to read without purpose and without satisfaction.

I have had people tell me that although they read the Bible, they stop short of Revelation—the final 'chapter'. Imagine! That particular Bible book announces itself as the Revelation of Jesus Christ. It forecasts the consummation of all things and introduces the new order. How can readers form a balanced understanding of God, sin, unbelief and divine judgement if they ignore so important a book? In these crisis days of world government, no Christian can afford to ignore the climactic Revelation.

We may take one of only two stances in regard to this prophetic 'unveiling'—this portraying of the future return of Jesus Christ to this earth, to this world that once rejected Him as Messiah and crucified Him at Calvary. We may ignore it, in effect despising it and jeering at the prospect of a future divine intervention affecting the entire world. Or we may embrace it, cheering for the promised victory of a righteous Ruler, the coming King of kings.

Those who ignore this book take their place with the many who believe a humanistic view of life is sufficient: that men and women are responsible captains of their own souls. They take their place with the defiant multitude who shout the age-old refrain: 'We will not have this man to rule over us!'

Those who take it seriously are convinced of an actual heavenly realm as real as the world we now inhabit.

They are persuaded that the day of consummation nears when 'the kingdom of the world' becomes 'the kingdom of our Lord and of his Christ', who 'will reign for ever and ever' (Rev 11:15).

God is sovereign

Living in this generation, we are fully aware that the competitive world and our selfish society have brought many new fears to the human race. I can empathise with those troubled beings who lie awake at night worrying about the possible destruction of the race through some evil, misguided use of the world's store of nuclear weapons. The tragedy is that they have lost all sense of the sovereignty of God! I, too, would not sleep well if I could not trust moment by moment in God's sovereignty and omnipotence and in His grace, mercy and faithfulness.

The prevailing attitudes of fear, distrust and unrest permeating our world are known to all of us. But in God's plan some of us also know a beautiful opposite: the faith and assurance found in the church of Jesus Christ. God still has a restful 'family' in His church. As believers we gladly place our confidence in God's Revelation of Himself. Although the material world has never understood our faith, it is well placed in the Scriptures. The Bible tells us many things we could learn in no other way.

This amazing Revelation—the final section of the holy Scriptures—tells us plainly that no human being and no world government or power will have any control or any say in that fiery day of judgement yet to come upon the earth. John's vision of things to come tells us clearly and openly that at the appropriate time the direction and administration of this world will be taken away from men and women and placed in the hands of the only man who has the wisdom and power to rightly govern. That man is the eternal Son of God, our Lord Jesus Christ.

Revelation describes the age-ending heavenly and earthly events when our Lord and Saviour is universally acknowledged to be King of kings and Lord of lords. All will acclaim Him victor. God's Revelation leaves us with no doubt about that.

In our present period of time, however, there is little recognition of God's sovereignty or of His plan for His redeemed people. Go into the market-place, into our educational institutions and—yes—even into our popular religious circles, and you will find a growing tendency to make mankind large and to make God small. Human society is now taking it for granted that if God indeed exists, He has become our servant, meekly waiting upon us for our will.

Believers are the true realists

In the face of this kind of human thinking, I want to make a case for the committed Christians in this world. We are the true realists. We confess that we do not hold the powers of life and death in our own hands. We have sensed the importance of John's vision in the Revelation. We are assured that God is alive and well and that He has never abdicated His throne. While others may wonder and speculate concerning God's place in the universe, we are assured that He has never yielded to any of His creatures His divine rights as Lord of man and nature.

It is for this reason that the Christian believer, related to God by faith, is assured of final victory. Even in the midst of earthly trials, he or she is joyful.

The unbeliever, who boastfully will 'take my chances', can only remain cynical. Deep within, he or she discovers doubts and uncertainties multiplying daily. Tell that person about this Revelation, about the certainty of Jesus Christ's ultimate victory, of God's promise of new heavens and a new earth, and he or she can only react with the cynic's biting contempt: 'Who cares about fables and empty promises? No person in his right mind would ever confess that he has been reading the book of Revelation!'

Take my word for it. Men and women who think they have all the answers about this life and the next have been mouthing their brave words for generations. They are big, challenging words, but they come from puny, empty hearts and minds. These infidels are too blind to recognise or acknowledge that God *does* have an eternal plan—a divine plan in which mankind is never permitted to utter the first word or the last.

The fact is that God has always been God—and He always will be God. He knows all about our human beginnings. He has had to consult with no one about anything!

One day that little bundle of delight, so fondly nurtured by parents and family, finds herself in human consciousness and accepts the fact that she *is*. It is at that point that her volitional life begins. Until that time, she had nothing to say about anything—absolutely nothing.

God will have the last word

Have you noticed, in the human family, how encouraged we are by the sound of our own voice? Men and women take to strutting and boasting, and in their pride they may declare their independence of God. Little do they realise that God in His divine sovereignty has reserved the right to take up at the last where He began at the first. It can mean only one thing: human beings are in the hands of God finally, whether they like it or not.

I declare this truth in all frankness because God's word, including the book of Revelation, tells us clearly that our man-made civilisations, so called, will not prevail in the coming day of judgement and consummation.

Secular-minded men and women seem annoyed by the premise that the Creator-God has in mind a plan for ending this age in which we live. They do not want to be told that organisations, governments and institutions cannot expect earthly things to continue as they are for ever and ever. Repeatedly and plainly the Bible tells us to expect Jesus, the Christ of God, to return to this earth in power and glory. People who have long joked about the 'invisibility' of the kingdom of God will see it established in righteousness and with authority.

Humans try to ignore God, continuing to make their own ambitious, selfish plans. In the years before the First World War, Germany's Kaiser Wilhelm, largely blamed for the beginning of the first world conflict, was exceedingly headstrong. At a chapel service attended by the kaiser, a faithful German minister preached on the coming again of Jesus Christ to establish God's kingdom of righteousness and peace throughout the earth. Wilhelm was greatly offended and spoke to the minister at the close of the service.

'I never want to hear that kind of a sermon again,' he

warned the preacher. 'Such an event is not at all in keeping with the plans we have for the future and glory of our fatherland!'

But Kaiser Wilhelm and, a generation later, Adolf Hitler are merely fading memories—illustrations of that vain human propensity to make ourselves big and God small.

There is vastly more in the Revelation than you or I will ever know while we are on this earth. But just God's urging that we be ready for the announced coming events should be sufficient to keep us expectant, interested—and praying!

The Revelation has to do with relationships

This Revelation of Jesus Christ has to do with His relationship to the Father, to the human race and to the church. It has to do with His relationship to Israel, to the nations, to our enemy the devil and to the coming judgement. Ministers faithful to the word of God have always said that Christ can be found on every page of the Bible. In the Revelation, we see Him dominating the eternal future. The message of the book is the almost overwhelming portrayal of Christ's victory, bringing about the final destruction of Satan and all of his works.

Part of our Christian restfulness comes from the fact that we are in the hands of a loving God who has already existed throughout all of the tomorrows. Because all time is in God, the flow of time never concerns God. He never has to run in an effort to catch up with the movement of time. The end of time is seen by God just as easily as the beginning of time.

That is why the Bible tells us that God knows the end from the beginning. That is why a godly man like John, caught up in the Spirit of God, could be shown the outline of future events. They were future to him, and they are future to us. That is because we are in the stream of time. They are not future to God because He is not in the stream of time.

The Revelation is the only New Testament book that may be classified as 'predictive' in its character and content. (It has been interesting to me to find in the writings of Blaise Pascal, the great seventeenth-century scientist and religious philosopher, his conclusion that no true prediction of mankind's future can be found anywhere but in the Christian Scriptures.)

About the predictive quality of the Scriptures we ought to be in agreement. If there cannot be any valid foresight, no revelation from God, nothing to warn us or prepare us for tomorrow, this life on earth would have to be considered a gloomy business indeed. Thankfully, we have a definite word, a promise upon which we can lean. Peter, one of God's special spokesmen, expressed it in this way:

> ...we have the word of the prophets made more certain, and you will do well to pay attention to it, as to a light shining in a dark place, until the day dawns and the morning star rises in your hearts. Above all, you must understand that no prophecy of Scripture came about by the prophet's own interpretation. For prophecy never had its origin in the will of man, but men spoke from God as they were carried along by the Holy Spirit.
>
> *2 Peter 1:19–21*

We may count on God's illumination

As Christian believers, we are assured that no matter how dark it becomes around us, God will faithfully pro-

vide the illumination of His Spirit. The Old Testament
offers in the release of Israel from Egyptian bondage a
fitting illustration. When God was moving toward the
climax of that deliverance, the darkness of night covered
Egypt, but, miraculously, there was light in the dwellings
of all of the Israelites. So, too, there is light even now for
us who are Christian believers concerning our future.
God's word is a light that shines in a dark place until the
morning star rises in our hearts.

Note, for your encouragement, that God has done
something special in the Revelation that He has done in
no other part of the New Testament. He has promised a
divine blessing for those who will read it:

> Blessed is the one who reads the words of this prophecy and
> blessed are those who hear it and take to heart what is
> written in it, because the time is near.
>
> *Rev 1:3*

This should be encouragement enough to read and consider what this book has to say. Although it is signifi-
cantly complex, the book is modest in size. There are but
twenty-two chapters, and none of them can be considered lengthy. A good reader can read through the book
in two or three hours.

God's message in Revelation, viewed as a whole, is a
prognosis of events affecting the entire created universe—'the things that must soon take place' (22:6).
Those who give themselves to its reading will sense they
are on a fast-moving guided tour, discerning a variety of
scenes and events in John's panoramic view of the
heavens and earth. In quick succession he takes us from
the highest heaven to the deepest hell. We hear the
trumpets sounding in heaven and see the woes and
judgements that follow upon the earth and its seas.

Instead of repenting, people harden their hearts against the God who created them and loved them.

John sees Jesus

John sees his Lord, Jesus Christ, in several different appearances. He is the dazzlingly radiant Son of Man with eyes like blazing fire (chapter 1). He is the victorious Lamb standing before the heavenly throne (chapter 5). He is the Conqueror on the white horse riding down the skies to the marriage supper of the Lamb (chapter 19). John also testifies to his vision of the sevenfold Spirit of God before the heavenly throne, whom he sees as seven blazing lamps (4:5).

As we read, we follow the spectacle of the suffering but triumphant church of Jesus Christ (chapters 7 and 19) and the divine seal set upon the righteous. John tells us of the Israel of that future day (chapter 7). He was profoundly impressed to see God's record books opened (chapter 20). John saw the 'synagogue of Satan' (2:9; 3:9), but before the vision ended, he foresaw the total defeat and chaining of Satan, his every power destroyed, his every licence taken away (20:1–3,7-10).

The Revelation is sobering, for it is a vision of judgement that is coming upon a sinful, selfish, violent world. John sees the Son of Man appearing with clouds to '[swing] his sickle over the earth' and reap the harvest (14:14–16). John must have been greatly moved as he viewed the new heaven and the new earth God is preparing for His people (21:1–5). He tells us of the river of life that flows for ever and, beside it, the tree of life with its leaves for the healing of the nations (22:1–2).

I speak of these things as still future. Many Christians of past centuries insisted that all the events and scenes in the Revelation were already history, that none of the book was predictive. It is a gracious aspect of our evangelical Christian fellowship that we do not make uniformity in prophetic interpretation the test of Christian orthodoxy. As believers we do not sit in judgement of others whose views on these matters are not identical with our own. Determining the actual day and hour of Christ's return to earth is not the occupation God has assigned to us. Our constant readiness to meet Him when He does return should be our most important consideration.

I have been studying these Scriptures for many years. I am prepared to give my answer to an ancient question: 'Are all these scenes in the Revelation history?' I can best answer with some questions of my own:

Has the sun yet turned black like sackcloth? Has the moon yet become blood red? Have the stars yet fallen from the heavens (6:12–13)?

Has there been a time when the sky receded like a scroll being rolled up? Have the mountains and the islands been moved from their places (6:14)?

When did the earth experience an invasion of locust-like creatures whose sting killed a third of the world's population (9:1–11)?

If the prophesied destroyer has already appeared and the seven angels of judgement have already done their work (chapters 8—9), would we not have known it?

Would there not be some notice in our history books if four specially commissioned angels and two hundred million extra-terrestrial cavalry had wiped out a third of earth's population (9:15–19)?

When was the abyss—that bottomless pit—opened to allow Satan to come forth again for a short time (20:7–8)?

No, I do not think all these events have taken place. On the other hand, I do believe that the word of God tells us we stand on the verge of the most dramatic and far-reaching developments since Adam stood up in the garden of Eden and Eve stood by his side. I do not know all the details of the future. But I do know that our Lord is returning to earth. And in that Day of our Lord, the Holy City will come down out of heaven beautifully dressed as a bride for her husband (21:2).

We have in the Scriptures many appeals to be ready for that day. We are not to live just for now and for this world. We are to live each day with a view of the world above! I am troubled because the church of Jesus Christ today does not seem to know as much about spiritual victory and rejoicing in the Lord as did our forefathers in the Christian faith and fellowship.

Within my own denominational background, I have read much and reflected often on the ministries of A.B. Simpson and the joyful fellowship of those who associated with him in the late years of the nineteenth century. One of the godly Christian brothers who joined with Dr Simpson was an officer in the Salvation Army, Russell Kelso Carter. He and those sincere believers were so enthralled with the scriptural promises of Christ's ultimate triumph that Carter was moved to write a gospel song that is still in our hymnal: *Jesus Is Victor!*

Congregations sang that message often in their services of praise, for they believed it was true. Jesus is Victor indeed! Kelso Carter's song depicts clearly and confidently the major themes that prevail throughout the book of Revelation:

Jesus is victor—His work is complete,
Crushing all enemies under His feet.

Jesus is victor; He died not in vain,
  Risen and glorified, Jesus doth reign!

Jesus is victor—without and within,
  Saving and keeping and cleansing from sin;
Jesus is victor, O heavenly Dove,
  Come to abide, and make perfect in love.

Jesus is victor—the heavens shall ring,
  Great king of terrors, where is thy sting?
Jesus is victor—we'll shout o'er the grave,
  Glory to God, He is mighty to save!

My word to you is this: Do not neglect, do not ignore God's message to our race in this Revelation of Jesus Christ.

2

The Prophecy—
I Am Coming Soon

Look, he is coming with the clouds,
and every eye will see him,
even those who pierced him;
and all the peoples of the earth will mourn because
   of him.
So shall it be! Amen.
   'I am the Alpha and the Omega,' says the Lord
God, 'who is, and who was, and who is to come, the
Almighty.'...
   'Behold, I am coming soon! Blessed is he who
keeps the words of the prophecy in this book.'...
   'Behold, I am coming soon! My reward is with
me, and I will give to everyone according to what he
has done. I am the Alpha and the Omega, the First
and the Last, the Beginning and the End.'...
   He who testifies to these things says, 'Yes, I am
coming soon.'
   Amen. Come, Lord Jesus.
                              Revelation 1:7–8; 22:7, 12, 20

The book of Revelation provides strong reinforcement
to the prophetic declaration of the other Christian Scrip-

tures: Jesus is coming again. The promise that the Creator God has a divine timetable for inaugurating a new order on this earth is not some novel idea advanced by over-zealous handlers of the Scriptures.

In evangelical churches there has always been an expectant hope of Christ's return to earth based on His own stated promises. The record is clear: many times during His earthly ministry, Jesus declared that He would come again to intervene in human history. From the first century of the Christian era to this present time, every generation of believers has expressed its hope for, and expectation of, Christ's return to earth. Wherever sincere Bible students turn in the New Testament, they find continual reminders that an overwhelming 'day of the Lord' is coming and that, in fact, it is imminent!

Who can ignore Jesus' own words on the subject?

> At that time the sign of the Son of Man will appear in the sky, and all the nations of the earth will mourn. They will see the Son of Man coming on the clouds of the sky, with power and great glory. And he will send his angels with a loud trumpet call, and they will gather his elect from the four winds, from one end of the heavens to the other....
>
> No-one knows about that day or hour, not even the angels in heaven, nor the Son, but only the Father.
>
> *Matthew 24:30, 31, 36*

The apostle Paul had similar words with the same significance for the believers in Thessalonica:

> You know very well that the day of the Lord will come like a thief in the night. While people are saying, 'Peace and safety,' destruction will come on them suddenly, as labour pains on a pregnant woman, and they will not escape.

But you, brothers, are not in darkness so that this day should surprise you like a thief.

1 Thessalonians 5:2–4

The apostle Peter wrote the same message of caution and spiritual preparation to the believers addressed in his second letter:

The day of the Lord will come like a thief. The heavens will disappear with a roar; the elements will be destroyed by fire, and the earth and everything in it will be laid bare.

Since everything will be destroyed in this way, what kind of people ought you to be? You ought to live holy and godly lives as you look forward to the day of God and speed its coming.

1 Peter 3:10–12

The Revelation ends with this brief message from the risen and glorified Christ: 'I am coming soon' (22:20). The message of the Revelation that Jesus, the Lamb alone found worthy, is the ultimate victor is closely intertwined with the outline of His return to earth as King of kings and Lord of lords.

We are responsible

I find myself often thinking about responsibility. It is sobering for us to realise that each generation of believers has had its own responsibility to be faithful to the Bible and its teachings. That responsibility includes the appeal of our Lord Jesus to watch and pray for the day of His return.

We must admit that many believers throughout the long centuries did become weary and discouraged. They concluded that the Lord was indeed delaying His return.

We have had a demonstration of this disinterest in our own Christian circles. There has been a definite decline in prophetic preaching and teaching. I am not alone in relating this decline to the excesses of preachers and teachers who were carried along by the moving tides of history during the First and Second World Wars. These teachers produced many exciting sermons and lectures, complete with colourful charts and books. Week after week they fed congregations with minute details of future events. They were dogmatic in insisting that the old Roman Empire was being restored before their eyes. Many of them regarded Mussolini, who had come to complete power in Italy, as the soon-to-be-revealed anti-christ described in the Bible.

They built up all of this to an ultimate climax that did not happen according to their predictions. They presumed to know more about the future than Daniel knew. They considered themselves wiser than Isaiah. They held themselves capable of seeing farther into the future than John the revelator. In a sense, many Christian were 'burned' by the extreme and forced interpretations of these would-be prophets. Just as a burned child fears the fire, so Christians of that era came to fear any further exposure to prophetic ideas or study.

Many yearn to be ready

There is no doubt in my mind, however, that millions of Christians in our day yearn within themselves to be ready to see the Lord when He appears. These are the saints of God who have a real understanding that what our Lord Jesus Christ *is to us* in our personal lives, moment by moment, is more important than merely dwelling always on what He *did for us*. A great segment

of Christian theology emphasises the utility of the cross on which Jesus died rather than the person who died on that cross for our sins.

It may surely be observed that most present-day Christians regard redemption as a kind of cut-and-dried commodity—a commodity they may obtain whenever their minds happen to turn to it. Thus, the entire spiritual transaction takes place without emotional content, without spiritual lift and assurance.

So, for many there is no emotional yearning for the return of Jesus. The best hope they know is a kind of intellectual, theological hope. But an intellectual knowledge of what the New Testament teaches about the return of Christ is surely a poor substitute for a love-inflamed desire to look on His face!

Right here, let me tell you that people have different motives for whatever interest they have in the prophetic Scriptures. Some are just curious—humanly curious! They look upon all the minor details of prophecy as the details of an amazing jigsaw puzzle. They will spend much time and effort trying to put the various pieces together, hoping to be the first to arrive at some new prophetic twist or surprising suggestion. But that motive is improper where the promises and claims of our Lord Jesus Christ are concerned. To approach this book of Revelation simply out of curiosity is, in my judgement, close to sacrilege. I liken it to the interest some might have in examining the cerement, or grave cloth, in which the body of our Lord was wrapped for burial, or in chemically analysing the blood that was shed for us on Calvary's cross.

Spiritual truth must be obeyed

In the spiritual realm, truth not acted on in obedience
becomes darkness. Our hearing the gospel, for example,
was not enough. Within our wills we had to act in faith
on God's saving truth. Without such action, we would
have been worse off for hearing; we would have added to
our guilt the sin of refusing to believe and obey God's
truth. So in matters of prophecy, shallow-minded,
inquisitive men and women should be warned that God
will make the light that is in them darkness if they
inquire only for the reason of curiosity.

The word of God is truly *the* word of God! We must
be careful concerning the motivation of our hearts. Let
us never be numbered with those who want to sniff
curiously at every truth without the least intention of
embracing and obeying what God has revealed.

But there is another kind of human curiosity now
prevalent among Bible students. It is the idea of 'finding
the key to the Scriptures'. Many are saying, 'I want to
find the key that will let me understand the Scriptures.' I
heard a Bible teacher on a radio broadcast promise his
listeners that he could give them the key to a proper
interpretation and understanding of the Bible. 'Of
course,' he added, 'you will have to write me and ask for
it.'

If we are serious Christian believers, we know that
there is no secret, magical key to unlock the meaning of
the Scriptures. God did not give us His word in the form
of a series of interlocking puzzle pieces, the solution
dependent upon our finding the proper key to allow
everything to fall into place.

No, the point cannot even be argued. The Holy Spirit
who in the first place inspired the Holy Writings is the
only one who can give us inner illumination as we read

and study the Bible. But people are human. They insist upon some easier way. 'If I can just find the key, I will have the understanding.'

It would be tempting, indeed, if we could approach the book of Revelation with so fascinating a prospect. 'Here is the key to Revelation. Whenever you want to enter the wonderful heavenly palace and take in all the scenes, just use this master key!' The faithful preachers and teachers would have a much different task if such a master key were available. They would not have to pray as much. They would not have to study and search as much. They would not have to meditate as much. They would not have to ask God for light and help. They would be able to spend much more of their time out on the lake matching wits with the fish.

We will not always agree about the details

I have already made it clear that our fellowship as Christian believers does not rest on our ability to agree concerning the interpretation of the prophetic Scriptures. Many of the acclaimed Christian saints of the past believed in the return of Christ to earth, but they did not necessarily adhere to what we now call the 'futurist' school of prophetic interpretation. In what I will have to say in this study of the Revelation, you may find yourself in disagreement with me. That is bound to happen as we explore these important issues. But we remain in fellowship despite such differences of opinion.

We do hold a common belief that Jesus is returning to earth, and that when He comes He will bring about the deathless, tearless kingdom He promised. No one knows the day or the hour of His coming. No one knows all the details of His coming or the exact progression of the events that mark His return. What, then, does God expect of us?

He wants us to continue to evidence love for one another, perhaps as we have never done so before. He wants us to worship Him together and to serve Him. He wants us to send this gracious gospel of Jesus Christ to the ends of the earth. All those things we can do even if our views about the rapture of the church, the great tribulation on earth or the details of Christ's return do not exactly coincide. We are blessed indeed if in regard to Christ's return we can say deep within ourselves, 'I am ready. I am prepared. I am among those longing to see Him face to face. Even so, come, Lord Jesus!'

That I have said this much about our spiritual freedom and about our fellowship in spite of differing views concerning the details of prophecy would rule me out of some churches. Years ago, during my ministry in Chicago, I was asked to speak to a well-known congregation across town. At the conclusion of my message I expressed the thought that all of us as Christians should live each day as though Christ might return at once, but we should work for our Lord as though He might not return for a thousand years.

I think the elderly layman who was asked to dismiss the meeting with prayer must have heard only my concluding words that we should work as though Christ might not return for a thousand years. In his prayer he told the Lord, on behalf of the congregation, that 'we did not get very much out of the sermon'. And during the rest of my years in Chicago, I did not receive another invitation to speak in that church! I could only assume that the leaders took it for granted that I was not expecting the return of the Lord for at least another millennium. And that ran counter to their understanding of things.

Actually, my message had centred on our being ready for Christ's return. I consider that the important emphasis. Christ's imminent return should underscore our need to be holy, joyful people, watching for that blessed hope.

As Christian believers who follow the Lamb, we are privileged to know the general outline concerning the end of the age and the arrival of the day of the Lord. The promise is that Christ will appear first to His waiting saints. In a twinkling of an eye, they will be changed, glorified and then caught up to be with Him. In that same instant, all of the righteous dead will be raised from their graves. All will be translated with the Lord Jesus to the wondrous site of the marriage supper of the Lamb.

In the view held by many, this translation of the saints is also the signal for the earth and its inhabitants to be plunged into the baptism of fire and blood known as the great tribulation. The battle of Armageddon will follow, and after that, Christ will return to earth in triumph to reign for a thousand years with His faithful and overcoming bride, the members of His glorified church.

Remember that we are God's believing and expectant people. We are not insects; we are the people of God. In faith we have the right and the privilege to rise from bended knee with faces turned to God, each of us gladly confessing, 'I belong to God through Jesus Christ, my Lord. I know that this whole world rightfully belongs to Jesus Christ, who is coming soon!'

The rightful owner will take over

The crux of the whole matter is this: our wonderful, created world will be restored to its rightful Owner. I for one look forward to that day. I want to live here when Jesus Christ owns and rules the world. Until that hour, there will be conflict, distress and war among the nations. We will hear of suffering and terror and fear and failure. But the God who has promised a better world is the God who cannot lie. He will shake loose Satan's hold on this world and its society and systems. Our heavenly Father will put this world into the hands that were once nailed to a cross for our race of proud and alienated sinners.

It is a fact. Jesus Christ is returning to earth. The Revelation teaches it. Daniel teaches it. Isaiah teaches it. Jeremiah teaches it. Go to the Gospels written by Matthew, Mark, Luke and John. They teach it. Read the promises in the Acts. Read them in Romans and the rest of Paul's epistles. Find the same message in Peter's important two letters to the churches. Jesus Christ is returning to earth!

The Scriptures inform us that Jesus Christ came once to die for our sins. He will come again to claim His redeemed people. He came once to go down under the steam-roller at man's feet. He will come again to renovate and restore the earth and to raise the righteous dead from the dust of their graves. I like Isaiah's expression of that coming day of resurrection and glorification:

> But your dead will live;
> their bodies will rise.
> You who dwell in the dust,
> wake up and shout for joy.
> *Isaiah 26:19*

We cannot even imagine the singing for joy and the shouts of victory when Christ comes for His own, when the righteous saints come forth in new and glorified bodies.

Surrounding the conference grounds at Glen Rocks, Ontario, are thousands and thousands of wild canaries— a part of the goldfinch family. They have always intrigued me. As long as they are feeding in large flocks, they are quiet and receive little attention. But stir them up with some kind of activity, and they all begin to sing together even as they fly away. That is my illustration— drawn from Isaiah's imagery. It is a picture of what the saints of God are going to do on the resurrection morning.

Rise and sing, you who dwell in the dust!

I bow my head and continue to pray with the humble writer of the Revelation: 'Amen! Come, Lord Jesus!'

3

The Appeal—Repent,
and Be Faithful

John,

To the seven churches in the province of Asia:

*Grace and peace to you from him who is, and
who was, and who is to come, and from the seven
spirits before his throne, and from Jesus Christ, who
is the faithful witness, the firstborn from the dead,
and the ruler of the kings of the earth.*

*To him who loves us and has freed us from our
sins by his blood, and has made us to be a kingdom
and priests to serve his God and Father—to him be
glory and power for ever and ever! Amen....*

*On the Lord's Day I was in the Spirit, and I
heard behind me a loud voice like a trumpet, which
said: 'Write on a scroll what you see and send it to
the seven churches: to Ephesus, Smyrna, Pergamum, Thyatira, Sardis, Philadelphia and
Laodicea.'*

Revelation 1:4–6, 10, 11

The glorified Christ instructed John: 'Write on a scroll
what you see and send it to the...churches.' The risen,
eternal Christ of God uses the vision He gave to His

servant John to transmit a message of warning and concern to every Christian congregation everywhere.

This call of Jesus to the Christian churches to prepare
themselves for His return finds its basis in the total
integrity of His promise. The Son of Man is a person of
His word. He said He would return, and He will. He will
return to earth and every eye will see Him. Further, all
the peoples of the earth will see Him. Further, all the
peoples of the earth will 'mourn' because of Him. It will
be a day of mourning, indeed, for those who did not
prepare—for those who refused to believe that He
meant what He said.

The more I study the Revelation, the more assured I
am that Christ's love for His church is unchanging and
eternal. We are barely into this Christ-centred prophecy
before Jesus signifies how important the church is to
Him.

Plainly, the living and eternal Head of the Christian
church was not asking for some outward show of human
perfection in His people. He was not appealing for a
merely formal and classic kind of churchmanship—
colourful pageantry, familiar ritual. Rather, His message
was an appeal for brotherly love, for spiritual warmth,
for genuine compassion. It was an expressed hope for
sincere repentance, for renewal, for faithfulness among
His forgiven, believing people, the children of God.

In the light of Christ's great love for His church, I
have tried to review my own concerns for the churches of
my pastoral ministry. I am aware that my critics say I
have spoken too freely and openly about apathy,
shallowness and worldliness in our Christian circles. I
have asked myself—and I again ask the critics: 'Are
words of warning, correction and reproof something new
in the Christian family?'

The question is rhetorical, of course. We already know the answer. It is an answer inherent in this divine message in the Revelation, addressed some nineteen hundred years ago to the Christian churches. The congregations named then have often been described as spiritually representative of all churches throughout the centuries of Christian history.

Enough rope for Satan

Before I pursue that theme, however, let me speak of Satan's big mistake. We have a familiar saying, 'Give a person enough rope and he will hang himself.' Satan must have congratulated himself when he succeeded in having John shut away in the lonely isolation of exile. But the plot boomeranged. Instead of getting an obituary notice announcing John's death, the churches received messages of great encouragement and the outline of Christ's future victory. Satan should never have stirred up the Roman authorities to arrest and banish the saintly John. God allowed His faithful disciple to see farther from his island prison than any king has been able to see from his palace!

John wrote what he saw and what he heard concerning the heavenly scene. He detailed the judgements of God that would ultimately take place on earth. The messages he conveyed to the churches were brief but significant. Many eminent Bible scholars through the years have expressed their belief that the spiritual mountains and valleys of Christian church history are portrayed in the divine descriptions of both spiritual life and spiritual drought at Ephesus, Smyrna, Pergamum, Thyatira, Sardis, Philadelphia and Laodicea.

This raises a question often asked: Why were these

messages directed to these seven churches? Why were
not some of the older churches—those in Jerusalem,
Antioch, Rome and Corinth, for instance—included?

We are finite, and we do not know the reasons. But
we do accept the fact that the Spirit of God was dictating
a special message that would ultimately convey God's
burden to the entire Christian community throughout
the world. And we know from its use elsewhere in the
Bible that the number *seven* suggests wholeness and
completeness. The fact that seven churches were
selected speaks of the possibility that the seven so named
were indeed representative examples of the entire
believing body of Christ on the earth.

They were familiar to John

These Asia Minor churches were especially dear to John.
No doubt he had assisted in their founding and for years
had lovingly nurtured their spiritual growth. There is
indication in extra-biblical sources that John had made
Ephesus his adopted city and in his home there had
cared for Mary, Jesus' mother, until her death.

What of the messages to these seven churches? Let us
consider their highlights.

To the church at Ephesus Jesus gave this word: 'You
have forsaken your first love. Remember the height from
which you have fallen!' (2:4–5). To Smyrna, Jesus had
this instruction: 'Be faithful, even to the point of death,
and I will give you the crown of life' (2:10).

Jesus had a rebuke for the church at Pergamum:
'Nevertheless, I have a few things against you....
Repent...!' (2:14,16). At Thyatira, wrong teaching and
evil conduct were to be repudiated. The Saviour said,
'...all the churches will know that I am he who searches

hearts and minds, and I will repay each of you according to your deeds' (2:23).

Jesus commanded the church at Sardis to rouse itself. 'I know your deeds; you have a reputation of being alive, but you are dead. Wake up!' (3:1–2). The one 'who is holy and true' had encouragement for the church in Philadelphia: 'Since you have kept my command to endure patiently, I will also keep you from the hour of trial that is going to come upon the whole world to test those who live on the earth' (3:10). His final message was to the church at Laodicea: 'I know your deeds, that you are neither cold nor hot.... So, because you are lukewarm—neither hot nor cold—I am about to spit you out of my mouth' (3:15–16).

From these brief summaries, it is apparent that even in that early period of church history, congregations were in need of reproof—and encouragement. Thankfully, a God of love and provision knows how to give both. In these messages we see the wise authority and loving direction of the Head of the church. In no better way could we be given a sweeping view of what Christianity is—and what the churches are all about.

Understanding Christianity

There are many definitions of Christianity in our day. Most of them are woefully weak because they lack the authority of God's revelation in His word. Christianity is not just another religious persuasion as defined by groups of religious leaders in Rome or Geneva, in New York City or Toronto. Christianity is actually what the Holy Spirit claimed it to be in the Scriptures. It is what the prophets of God, the seers and sages and apostles said it was as they were moved by the Holy Spirit to speak and to write.

This is the Christian life and Christian witness we accepted when we became Christians by sincere faith in God's word. Here is the beating heart of the holy faith that will take us home to heaven and to God. Here is our heart interest and here is our hope for the eternal future.

As John portrays the true meaning of the Christian faith in the churches, he relates everything to God, the Father, who was and who is and who is to come; to the sevenfold Spirit of God who proceeds from the Father; and to Jesus Christ, the eternal Son, our Saviour and Lord. The entire declaration to the churches rings with the certainty of the ultimate triumph to come.

Although there is enough spiritual and doctrinal teaching in these first three chapters of the Revelation for a dozen books, I want at this time to emphasise just two things: (1) the divine authority given to our Lord Jesus Christ and (2) the power and the illumination the church needs to receive from the Holy Spirit. I will also briefly mention a doctrine that is not always recognised: the dominion of the saints—really, the authority given to the believing children of God.

First of all, John mentions the two treasures, grace and peace, that God has willed to those who believe and obey (1:4). He designates grace and peace as coming to us, men and women in fellowship with God. John makes a benediction of these two spiritual treasures. Then he fashions a wonderful doxology: to Jesus Christ belongs 'glory and power for ever and ever' (1:6).

Benediction literally means 'the good word'. *Doxology* means 'the word of praise'. Taken together, the two put things in their right places: grace and peace for us believing men and women; glory and power for the God who has loved us to the point of death. What a frightful, grotesque situation it would be both in heaven and on earth if those roles were reversed! We cannot imagine a time and situation in which our God would need grace and peace—or in which we humans should be accorded glory and power for ever and ever.

No, the roles and the positions are correctly stated. Why would we ever need more for our wretched sinfulness than the grace of God? What more do we need for our poor, uprooted, alienated, distraught souls than peace?

Beyond grace and peace: love

The Holy Spirit then helps us recognise the kind of love we received from Jesus Christ, who has freed us from our sins by His blood. Have you yet learned that love is not a thing of reason? Love tries to be reasonable, but it seldom succeeds. There is a sweet wisdom in love that is above reason—it rises above it and goes far beyond it. Who could ever imagine the God of all the universe condensing Himself into human form and, out of His love, dying for His alienated people? It seems an unreasonable thing to do, but it was reasonable in that it was the supreme wisdom of the mighty God!

The saintly lady who was known as Julian of Norwich, centuries ago, cherished this love that is ours in Christ. She wrote: 'Out of His goodness, God made us. Out of His goodness, He keeps us. When man had sinned, He redeemed us again out of His goodness. Then do you not suppose that God will give His children the best of everything out of His goodness?'

But on to the divine authority ascribed to Jesus Christ, the eternal Son. Three things are said of Him here. He is the faithful witness, which means He is God's prophet. He is the firstborn from the dead, which speaks of His priesthood. And He is the ruler of the kings of the earth, which implies His kingship. This is the ageless revelation from God concerning His Christ. Jesus our Lord is Prophet, Priest and King. The concept is not new, yet many preachers never preach it and many congregations never hear it.

Jesus was God's faithful witness. In effect He said: 'I am a reporter. I have come down from heaven, and the things that I saw there I speak to you. I tell you the truth, but you will not receive it.' He was the Prophet of all prophets, the summation of all of God's prophets.

But He was more. His ministry was that of the priest of God. He offered Himself. He was the only priest in all of history who could offer Himself as an offering and a sacrifice to God. The writer to the Hebrews says clearly that 'Christ . . . through the eternal Spirit offered himself unblemished to God' (9–14). Then God raised Him from the dead, and He is now our great High Priest at the right hand of God

> Where high the heavenly temple stands,
> The house of God not made with hands,
> The great High Priest our nature wears,
> The Guardian of mankind appears.

Jesus is a glorified man

Let this truth penetrate. There is a glorified human being at the right hand of God—not a spirit but a man glorified. He is there interceding for us, representing us. This is why I believe in the security of the saints. How can I help but believe that? If Jesus Christ is at the right

hand of God, then He has invested Himself—charged
Himself—with full authority, authority given Him by
God the Father. My name is on His multi-stone breast-
piece (see Exodus 39:8–14), and I am safe!

Someone once asked Dr Graham Scroggie, 'Are you a
Calvinist?' I feel Dr Scroggie was speaking for me when
he replied, 'When I am on my knees praying, I am a
Calvinist. But when I get into the pulpit to preach, I am
an Arminian!' That my great High Priest will keep me, I
have no doubt. Will He do so because of my goodness?
No! Will He keep you because of your goodness? Again,
no! We are kept because He is at the throne of God
interceding for us.

Jesus Christ is also Ruler over all the kings of the
earth, and we await His day of consummation and triumph when every knee shall bow before Him 'in heaven
and on earth and under the earth, and every tongue
confess that Jesus Christ is Lord, to the glory of God the
Father' (Philippians 2:10–11).

A question for the church

There is a question that should be answered in every
Christian church: Are we honouring the Holy Spirit of
God? That is, are we allowing Him to do what He wants
to do in our midst today?

More than once in the Revelation John mentions the
sevenfold Spirit of God and His presence before the
heavenly throne. In the Old Testament, the prophet
Isaiah describes his stirring vision of this same Spirit,
who was to be God's presence, wisdom, understanding,
counsel, might, knowledge and reverence in the life of
the expected Messiah (Isaiah 11:1–3). Jesus did not begin

His earthly ministry until at His water baptism the living Spirit of God had become all of those things to Him.

I have reason to suspect that many people are trying to give leadership in Christian churches today without ever having yielded to the wise and effective leading of the Holy Spirit. He truly is the Spirit of wisdom, understanding and counsel. He alone can bring the gracious presence of the living God into our lives and ministries.

You may think it out of place for me to say so, but in our churches today we are leaning too heavily upon human talents and educated abilities. We forget that the illumination of the Holy Spirit of God is a necessity, not only in our ministerial preparation, but in the administrative and leadership functions of our churches.

We need an enduement of the Spirit of God! We sorely need more of His wisdom, His counsel, His power, His knowledge. We need to reverence and fear the Almighty God. If we knew the full provision and the spiritual anointing that Jesus promised through the Holy Spirit, we would be far less dependent on so many other things.

Psychiatrists, psychologists, anthropologists, sociologists—and most of the other 'ologists'—have their place in our society. I do not doubt that. But many of these professionals now have credentials in the church, and I fear that their counsel is put above the ministry of the Holy Spirit. I have said it before, and I say it now: We need the Holy Spirit more and more, and we need human helps less and less!

We shall have dominion

There is a further beautiful emphasis within John's opening benediction and ascription of praise to God. We

identify it as the doctrine of the dominion of the saints.
John says this eternal Prophet, Priest and King not only
'has freed us from our sins by his blood', but in addition
He 'has made us to be a kingdom and priests to serve his
God and Father' (1:5–6). We have greater authority
than we know—and greater authority than we ever
exercise!

There is an amazing provision for Christian believers
in our daily encounters and conflicts with Satan, the
enemy of our souls. I cannot agree with those optimistic
people who try to dismiss Satan as a figment of the
imagination. They are wrong. There is a real devil. But
we do not have to be afraid of him if we know and
exercise the dominion and authority of the saints of God.

The Bible tells us that Satan is a real personality. He
has a distinct history behind him. We dare to face and
resist him in the authority that comes to us from heaven.
John tells us that our authority comes from Jesus Christ,
who has made His believing saints to be a kingdom and
priests in His service.

God holds no mental reservations about any of us
when we become His children by faith. When He for-
gives us, He trusts us as though we had never sinned.
When Satan comes around to taunt me about my past
sins, I remind him that everything that had been charged
against me came from him, and now everything I have—
forgiveness and peace and freedom—I have freely
received from my Lord Jesus Christ!

As long as you remain on this earth, God has not
completed His work in you. The Spirit of God will help
you discern when the chastening hand of God is upon
you. But if it is the devil trying to tamper with your
Christian life and testimony, dare to resist him in the
victorious power of the living Christ.

This great truth is related to the fact that Jesus is our eternal High Priest, now exalted at the throne of God. He has said to us, 'Whatever your need, just come to the throne of grace. Anything you need, you may have!' Why not believe Him and exercise the dominion He has given you?

There is no reason for any of us to hide or to slink about as if we must get permission to exist. As children of God, we need not apologise for walking around in God's earth. Christ has made us a kingdom of believer-priests. We have the right as believer-priests to go direct to our great High Priest in the heavens, making our legitimate wants and wishes known to Him. He has promised to intercede for us at the heavenly throne.

Why do so few respond?

The dominion of the saints is an encouraging, uplifting truth. Why, then, does not everyone know about it and respond? Indeed, why do millions of men and women not respond to the grace and love of God? Has 'the god of this age... blinded the minds of unbelievers, so that they cannot see the light of the gospel of the glory of Christ' (2 Corinthians 4:4)?

The proponents of universalism twist certain Bible verses to make them the saving umbrella for the whole human race. But Scripture forbids such a conclusion, and reason forbids it. The promises are for the Lord's people—for those who are His by faith, those who love and serve Him.

There is no other way than the faith way. Everyone—every man and every woman—must decide whether he or she will be included under this gracious benediction from God the Father or excluded from claiming it!

4

The Portrait—
the Eternal Christ

*I, John, your brother and companion in the suffer-
ing and kingdom and patient endurance that are
ours in Jesus, was on the island of Patmos because
of the word of God and the testimony of Jesus....*

*I turned round to see the voice that was speaking
to me. And when I turned I saw seven golden lampstands, and among the lampstands was someone
'like a son of man,' dressed in a robe reaching down
to his feet and with a golden sash round his chest.
His head and hair were white like wool, as white as
snow, and his eyes were like blazing fire. His feet
were like bronze glowing in a furnace, and his voice
was like the sound of rushing waters. In his right
hand he held seven stars, and out of his mouth came
a sharp double-edged sword. His face was like the
sun shining in all its brilliance....*

*'The mystery of the seven stars that you saw in my
right hand and of the seven golden lampstands is
this: The seven stars are the angels of the seven
churches, and the seven lampstands are the seven
churches.'*

Revelation 1:9, 12–16, 20

All of the great artists of the past, all of them combining their talents on a gigantic canvas, could never have given us a true portrait of our Lord Jesus Christ or of His universal power. Instead, we look into the Scriptures, and particularly into the Revelation, to find a satisfying description of the eternal Son of God with whom we will be associated throughout the ages to come.

William T. MacArthur, an early leader in The Christian and Missionary Alliance and one of its outstanding preachers, termed the description of Jesus Christ in 1:13– 16 'the only authentic portrait of our Saviour and Lord'.

Those celebrated European painters, whose works adorn the world's great art galleries, undoubtedly did their best to depict our Lord. They were limited, however, by their finite concepts of the subject. To be frank, I do not want to hold in my mind an unworthy concept of my divine Saviour. We Christians should earnestly desire the Holy Spirit to sketch a true and transforming portrait of Jesus Christ across our innermost beings! Our delight should be in the assurance that Christ lives within us, moment by moment. And that assurance must come from God's holy word.

Do you personally desire with me that the Holy Spirit will dip His brush and begin to paint across the canvas of our souls a living portrayal of Jesus Christ, complete with blood and fire?

It is a sad thought, but I suppose some Christians are going to be disappointed when they actually see Jesus. Their concept of Him has been shaped by the paintings and images they have seen of the human Jesus. The radiant, awesome Jesus of the Revelation is totally outside their perspective.

Those who are critical of the Scriptures would have us believe that the symbols in this book are meaningless and a study in futility. I take strong exception to such conclusions! John saw much, he learned much, and he shares his understanding. For example, Jesus explained to John that the seven stars in His right hand are the angels of the seven churches. John passes on that information to us.

Valuable insights

In detailing his vision of the risen, glorified Christ, John conveys valuable insights to us. Jesus' vesture is the priestly robe. His golden sash is designed for royalty. His snow-white head and hair speak of God's utter holiness. His eyes, 'like blazing fire', and his feet, 'like bronze glowing in a furnace', depict God's wrath and judgement. John saw the face of Jesus as the sun shining in its full strength. How can anyone add to that? If you want to know how strong the sun is, try looking into the sky at midday. You never, never can gaze directly into that full glow.

But we are Jesus' disciples, and we think of another time and another scene when Jesus' 'appearance was so disfigured beyond that of any man and his form marred beyond human likeness' (Isaiah 52:14). It was a time when 'he had no beauty or majesty to attract us to him, nothing in his appearance that we should desire him' (Isaiah 53:2).

Yes, this Jesus Christ had come to live among us and to give His life a ransom for the sins of a lost world. Evil men took Him and said, 'We know how to deal with Him.' They beat Him with their whips and bruised Him with their fists. They tore at His beard, leaving His countenance marred and bleeding. In final insult, they spit in His holy face. Yet, as He bled and died on a

Roman cross, He cried out in prayer, 'Father, forgive
them, for they do not know what they are doing' (Luke
23:34).

As one of the redeemed and forgiven, I can better
understand Isaiah's portrait of the suffering Saviour, the
Servant of Jehovah. I know He was willing to die in my
place. But in John's vision, Jesus is the overcomer, the
one who was dead but now is alive for ever and ever. I
cannot fully comprehend the power and the glory
belonging to this one whose face will shine eternally with
the brilliance of the sun! I do not have the words to
explain that kind of brightness and light.

Jesus created everything

Our scientists explain to us how the sun daily gives us
light, heat and health, all the while providing energy and
a variety of necessary elements that are absorbed into
the earth. Then we dig and probe to release the oil, gas
and coal that the sun has helped to make. We put them
in our combustion chambers so that our cars and trains
and ships and planes can traverse the world.

John portrays the man who made it all, the one whose
face shines with the brilliance and energy of the sun.
'The man who made it all?' you ask, puzzled. Yes! Hear
what the apostle Paul says of Jesus Christ: 'He is the
image of the invisible God, the firstborn over all creation. For by him all things were created: things in
heaven and on earth, visible and invisible, whether
thrones or powers or rulers or authorities; all things were
created by him and for him' (Colossians 1:15–16).

Some may doubt this fact, but for the gospel's sake—
and because Scripture clearly states it—we must assert
that they are wrong. We must stand up to those who

would belittle Jesus Christ. We must take issue with those who question that John saw and tried to describe the eternity, the majesty, the glory, the power and the final authority of Jesus Christ, our Lord. As for me, I am positive about this Revelation God has given to His believing children!

No stranger to suffering

John was well aware of Satan's attack against God and the church in that first century of Christian history. He humbly affirmed that he was a 'companion in the suffering . . . and patient endurance that are ours in Jesus' (1:9). And what had John's faithful Christian testimony earned for him? Exile!

Had it happened in the West in our era, some publisher would have flown in to offer John a five- or six-figure cheque for book rights to his story. But I do not think John would have been concerned about turning a personal financial profit from his experience. The present-day financial value of a 'born again testimony' was mercifully unknown in AD 95.

'Give your heart to the Lord, get born again, and your business will grow and grow!' 'If you want to become a top athlete and be well known, just accept the Lord and be born again!' 'If you want your cows to give more milk . . .' 'If you want to be sure of getting better grades in college . . .'

Possibly no one ever had a clearer, sweeter, stronger testimony of the grace and salvation that is in Jesus Christ than John. Humbly he relates it: 'I . . . [am] your brother and companion in . . . suffering . . . [I] was on the island of Patmos because of the word of God and the testimony of Jesus.'

In our day, the media would be asking, 'What are you doing there on Patmos, John? You were the bishop at Ephesus. You should be at home among your people, presiding over your congregation. You were born again, were you not, John?'

'Yes,' John would have replied meekly, 'I was the Lord's disciple and companion, and I have been ministering and witnessing as He said. I am now His servant in exile.'

Allow me to be frank about this insidious issue in our Christian circles. If the modern doctrine of 'accepting Jesus' is all its current advocates claim it to be, John would not have been suffering in a one-man slave camp on Patmos. He would be at home with his congregation. He would have financial prosperity. He would know what strings to pull and how to be friendly with the right people in high places.

But no Revelation

Remember this, however: If John had been a product of our present-day 'accept Jesus and prosper' gospel, he would have seen no divine vision of Christ's glory and coming triumph; he would have written no Revelation. John could have chosen to compromise his faith. Had he done so, he would have remained at home—balancing his praise between God and Caesar. But then he never would have glimpsed that open door in heaven or the throne with the heavenly rainbow encircling it.

Yes, John could have taken the easier way. Just a little compromise and the important people would begin to say, 'This man is really doing good things for the community.' But John was a man of faith. He knew *what* he believed; he knew *in whom* he believed. He was willing to take the heat from those who hated the living God and His Christ.

If you are willing to lower the temperature of your testimony, the world will turn off the heat it has been applying. But if you are faithful to God and His word, consistent and sincere in your testimony to what Christ means to you, you can expect both heat and pressure. John had a strong, uncompromising testimony. It evoked the opposition of the powers, who decided to silence his witness in Patmos's rocky isolation.

There is a spiritual lesson for us in John's response to the voice of the living Christ. He says, 'I turned round to see the voice that was speaking to me' (1:12). John was not the first person to hear the Lord's voice behind him. Does this say to us that we are usually facing the wrong way?

The prophet Isaiah knew full well that Israel had turned its back on God, departing from His way. He counselled, 'Whether you turn to the right or to the left, your ears will hear a voice behind you, saying, "This is the way; walk in it" (Isaiah 30:21). Let us be thankful for God's mercy and patience. He is the only one who is always faithful, always loyal, always compassionate. His voice continues to call, 'Come! Turn back! Walk in My way!'

John says he turned and 'saw...someone "like a son of man"'. His vision was that of our Lord and His presence in the midst of the churches. In our time we have all kinds of status symbols in the Christian church—membership, attendance, pastoral staff, missionary offerings. But there is only one status symbol that should make a Christian congregation genuinely glad. That is to know that our Lord is present, walking in our midst!

Our real need

Some Christians say they need a great cathedral if they
are to properly worship—or a mighty organ or artistic,
stained-glass windows. Do not be concerned about those
outward symbols. Just be sure you have gladly welcomed
into your midst the one whose eyes are like a flame of
fire, the one from whose mouth proceeds a double-edged
sword—the word of God.

Some time ago I was invited to visit and preach in a
smaller church in Toronto. I found a group of dear
people—a humble, ethnic assembly. Many of them
could not speak good, standard English. But their faith
and joy in knowing Christ warmed my heart. After the
service, they called for a prayer meeting, and I want to
tell you that it was an experience I will never forget!

No matter the size of the assembly or its other
attributes, our Lord wants it to be known by His presence in the midst. I would rather have His presence in
the church than anything else in all the wide world.

Hearing the proud manner in which some speak of the
high cost of their sanctuaries must lead people to suppose that spirituality can be purchased. But the secret of
true spiritual worship is to discern and know the presence of the living Christ in our midst.

One further thought: John turned and saw 'someone
"like a son of man"' in the midst of the churches. John
did not see a spirit. He saw a man—a glorified man, the
Son of Man, our Lord Jesus Christ, clad in a priestly
garment and wearing the golden sash of royalty. He was
not a spirit, not an angel, not a cherubim. He was a real
man—a priest with royal insignia, bringing to mind
again the designation of the eternal Son as Prophet,
Priest and King. He stands in the midst of the churches.

Does that not explain much about the life and faithfulness of Christian churches? Many have their difficulties. Many have known the path of backsliding. Satan brings his pressures to bear on weaknesses in the church. If it were not for the presence of our Lord and Saviour in the midst, there would be no church! God's presence is the only reason for its existence.

In John's portrayal, the Son of Man had feet like bronze, glowing as if in a fire. This is the language and symbolism of judgement, and our Lord is to be Judge. The church that accepts no judgement is not the church of our Lord Jesus Christ. It cannot be Christ's church if our risen and glorified Lord is not the centre of all its interests.

The church must be holy

The true church understands that it must live a disciplined life. Although our High Priest loves us in spite of our weaknesses and failures, He encourages us to be a holy people because He is a holy God. Holiness may be an unpopular subject in some churches, but holiness in the Christian life is a precious treasure in God's sight.

What I say here may hurt, but I say it anyhow. We have lived with unholiness so long that we are almost incapable of recognising true holiness. The people of God in the churches of Jesus Christ ought to be a holy people. But ministers have largely given up preaching Bible-centred sermons on holiness. Maybe they would not know what to do with hearers who fell under the convicting power of God's word. Preachers today would rather give their congregations tranquillisers.

I preach to my congregation week after week. And I pray that I may be able to preach with such convicting power that my people will sweat! I do not want them to

leave my services feeling good. The last thing I want to
do is to give them some kind of religious tranquilliser—
and let them go to hell in their relaxation.

The Christian church was designed to make sinners
sweat. I have always believed that, and I still believe it.
The messages preached in our churches should make
backslidden Christians sweat. And if I achieve that
objective when I preach, I thank God with all of my
heart, no matter what people think of me.

Our Lord is a holy Lord, and His eyes are as a flame
of fire. His X-ray eyes can see right through everything!
We can hide nothing from God. He sees all and knows
all. But apparently we have a hard time with that fact—
preachers and lay people alike. We seem to think our
respectability should be accepted by our Lord as spirituality. That is the same tragic mistake the self-right-
eous Pharisees made in Jesus' day. We like to imagine
we are important, and we like to hear people talking
about our importance. But every one of us is going to die
one of these days. There will be a funeral service and
then we will be buried, just like everybody else.

God already knows all about us

God knows everything about me better than I know it
myself. He knows that my humility is only another form
of pride. He knows that! And I am glad He does. Some
people have an idea the devil may tattle some scandal
about them to God. They forget that God already knows
all there is to know about them.

I am glad God knows all He knows. No one is going to
seek out our Lord and whisper behind his or her hand,
'Have you heard the latest about Tozer?' Jesus already
knows everything there is to know about me. He knows

my strengths and He knows my weaknesses. And He has already told us that the only thing capable of harming us is to believe we can do all things in our own strength.

We can never get too weak for the Lord to use us—but we can get too strong, if it is our own strength. We can never be too ignorant for the Lord to use us—but we can be too wise in our own conceit. We can never get too small for the Lord to use us, but we can surely get too big and get in His way.

The Christian church dares not settle for anything less than the illumination of the Holy Spirit and the presence of our divine Prophet, Priest and King in our midst. Let us never be led into the mistake that so many are making—sighing and saying, 'Oh, if we only had bigger, wiser men in our pulpits! Oh, if we only had more important men in places of Christian leadership!'

In John's vision, the sharp, double-edged sword proceeded out of the mouth of the Son of Man. All other swords will fail and vanish, but the sharp sword, the word of the Lord, will prevail. By all means, we had better stay with the sharp sword of His word.

How terrible it is to simply go on playing in God's presence. How human it is to sleep and dream in God's presence. What a tragedy when we sin in His presence. Jesus our Lord is in our midst. He is here. Now. And we are a people getting ready to see Him face to face.

Are we ready for that face-to-face encounter?

5

The Call to Worship—
Holy, Holy, Holy

After this I looked, and there before me was a door standing open in heaven. And the voice I had first heard speaking to me like a trumpet said, 'Come up here, and I will show you what must take place after this.' At once I was in the Spirit, and there before me was a throne in heaven with someone sitting on it. . . . Also in front and behind the throne there was what looked like a sea of glass, clear as crystal.

In the centre, around the throne, were four living creatures, and they were covered with eyes, in front and behind. The first living creature was like a lion, the second was like an ox, the third had a face like a man, the fourth was like a flying eagle. Each of the four living creatures had six wings and was covered with eyes all around, even under his wings. Day and night they never stop saying:

> *'Holy, holy, holy*
> *is the Lord God Almighty,*
> *who was, and is, and is to come.'*

Whenever the living creatures give glory, honour

*and thanks to him who sits on the throne and who
lives for ever and ever, the twenty-four elders fall
down before him who sits on the throne, and worship him who lives for ever and ever. They lay their
crowns before the throne and say:*

> *'You are worthy, our Lord and God,
> to receive glory and honour and power,
> for You created all things,
> and by your will they were created
> and have their being.'*

Revelation 4:1–2, 6–11

What a moving thought it is to learn that in the heavenly
realm God receives unceasing worship from the living
creatures surrounding His throne!

Day and night they never stop saying:

> 'Holy, holy, holy
> is the Lord God Almighty,
> who was, and is, and is to come.'
> *Revelation 4:8*

As John glimpsed the majesty and holiness of God in
this heavenly scene, he was overwhelmed by what he saw
and heard. It must have been like trying to pour an
ocean into a teacup—and John staggered under the
revelation! He had to try to describe the indescribable,
and he lacked both language and reference points to do
so. But he recognised the unceasing worship ascribed to
God the Father around His heavenly throne.

Looking at what John wrote, I wonder how so many
present-day Christians can consider an hour of worship

Sunday morning as adequate adoration of the holy God who created them and then redeemed them back to Himself. I have been at funerals where the presiding minister preached the deceased right into heaven. Yet the earthly life of the departed plainly said that he or she would be bored to tears in a heavenly environment of continuous praise and adoration of God.

This is personal opinion, but I do not think death is going to transform our attitudes and disposition. If in this life we are not really comfortable talking or singing about heaven, I doubt that death will transform us into enthusiasts. If the worship and adoration of God are tedious now, they will be tedious after the hour of death. I do not know that God is going to force any of us into His heaven. I doubt that He will say to any of us, 'You were never interested in worshipping Me while you were on earth, but in heaven I am going to make that your greatest interest and your ceaseless occupation!'

Controversial? Perhaps. But I am trying to stir you up, to encourage you to delight in a life of praise and spiritual victory! God is pleased with His people when His praise is continually and joyfully on their lips. The heavenly scene John describes is the unceasing cry of the adoring living creatures, 'Holy, holy, holy!' They rest not, day or night. My fear is that too many of God's professing people down here are resting far too often between their efforts at praise.

The elders and the 'creatures'

Turning again to John's vision, we learn that surrounding the throne of God were twenty-four other thrones, and seated on them were twenty-four elders. They were dressed in white robes, and they had crowns of gold on their heads. Then John describes four 'living creatures' covered with eyes, each having six wings. John says that when these four living creatures ascribe glory, honour and thanks to God, the twenty-four elders fall down before God and worship Him. The elders lay their crowns before the throne and say, 'You created all things. You are worthy to receive glory and honour and power.'

Do we know the symbolism of these twenty-four elders? No. The Scriptures do not make it clear. But I am going to tell you how I have come to view these worshipping elders. I think twelve of them probably represent the overcomers in Israel and twelve of them represent the overcomers in the church. To say it another way, twelve represent the twelve tribes of Israel; twelve represent the twelve apostles of Jesus Christ.

Do you recall Peter's remark during one of his conversations with Jesus? 'We have left everything to follow you! What then will there be for us?' (Matthew 19:27). Jesus responded with this statement: 'I tell you the truth, at the renewal of all things, when the Son of Man sits on his glorious throne, you who have followed me will also sit on twelve thrones, judging the twelve tribes of Israel' (Matthew 19:28). The thrones Jesus mentions may not be the ones John saw, but Jesus' words were certainly definite about the apostles sitting on twelve thrones in that coming day.

John also saw four 'living creatures'. You may recall that they were termed 'beasts' in the King James Version. I think 'living creatures' is a better translation because they were not 'beastly' creatures. Again, we sympathise with John as he tries to describe heavenly creatures in human terms. It was impossible for God to fully reveal Himself and the heavenly glories to John.

How can the Infinite be fully perceived by finite, mortal man?

God had to impose some sort of a veil. If God had suddenly revealed Himself fully to John, the apostle would have perished as an autumn leaf disappears in a blazing fire. No mortal can look into the blaze of God's full glory and live! So John is attempting to tell us what he discerns in the vision of the four heavenly beings at the throne of God.

The four living creatures

The first living creature was like a lion. The second was like an ox. The third had the face of a man. The fourth was like a soaring eagle. Lion—king of beasts. Ox—beast of burden. Man—what *we* are. Flying eagle—at home in the heavens. Do you perceive a larger picture developing? Did you know that for centuries Christians have seen these same 'faces' in the four Gospels of the New Testament? Matthew's is the Gospel of the King. Mark's, the Gospel of the suffering Servant. Luke's, the Gospel of the Son of Man. John's, the Gospel of the Son of God.

God has put Jesus Christ's picture everywhere! Four living, immortal creatures before the throne. Four loving, adoring, worshipping beings, faithfully and for ever devoted to the purpose of praising God and the eternal Son, the Lamb of God who takes away the sin of the world!

Make no mistake about it. The imagery is plainly the gospel of Christ. He is what Christianity is all about.

The characteristics of the lion are power and dominion. The lion is *king*. The glory of a king does not lie in his own person but rather in the character of his people.

The glory of this noble and kingly person, Christ Jesus,
pictured as the lion, lies in the fact that He rules a people
who are supremely and perfectly happy.

The ox is the willing burden-bearer, obedient even to
sacrifice. In the Old Testament system, there was little
for the ox to look forward to except sacrifice, blood and
death. The ox is a symbol of God's great plan of atone-
ment and redemption through Jesus Christ.

The third being, John testified, had a face like a man.
The symbolism of the Son continues, for Jesus became
man and lived among us that He might die for us: '. . . the
Son of Man did not come to be served, but to serve, and
to give his life as a ransom for many' (Mark 10:45).

Finally, the eagle-like fourth living creature was a
flying, soaring being. earth may be the eagle's resting
place, but the heavens are its habitat. Jesus was the Son
of Man, partaking of our humanity, but He was also the
Son of God—'very God of very God', as the fathers
phrased it in the Nicene creed.

Are we walking in the light?

What have we been doing with all the light and guidance
God has given us in His word and through His Spirit? I
am concerned that some Christian leaders are deriding
the 'mysticism' of spiritually minded Christian
believers—men and women who are so devoted to Jesus
Christ that nothing else in this life and in this world much
matters.

A couple of generations ago, all Christendom was in
one of two camps: People were either 'liberals' (also
called 'modernists' and 'rationalists'), who questioned
the inspired authority of the Scriptures and who denied
that Jesus was more than a master teacher and a splendid

human example, or they were 'evangelicals'—accepting without question the fundamental and total authority of the Scriptures as God's Spirit-inspired word and recognising Jesus Christ as God embodied in flesh. Now, suddenly, we find the lines are no longer so simply drawn. Now an increasing number of scholars and authors claim to be both evangelicals and rationalists.

Church history is clear. Jesus Christ has always had devoted, adoring followers who found it possible to love their Saviour and Lord with all their hearts and minds and souls. If so-called evangelicals can now speak lightly about these 'evangelical mystics', we must conclude that truth in our day has taken a cruelly cynical twist.

Those evangelical mystics have been a potent force for God and for the word of God. You will have to count Moses, David, Isaiah, John and Paul among them. You will have to count Augustine, Luther and the Wesleys. You will have to add Julian of Norwich, Fanny Crosby, Francis Faber, Brother Lawrence, A.B. Simpson and a mighty host of other men and women whose greatest delight in life was the rapturous love of God in their souls!

Could it be that in our advanced generation we are forgetting that all people will have to answer to God for the decisions they made in life either accepting or rejecting the spiritual light God has given them? Are we forgetting that the moral judgements of God will fall upon individuals and nations according to the light they have received?

Degrees of punishment

The Bible is plain: 'That servant who knows his master's will and does not get ready or does not do what his

master wants will be beaten with many blows. But the
one who does not know and does things deserving
punishment will be beaten with few blows' (Luke 12:47–
48). God is a merciful God, but He is also holy and just.
I do not believe, as some do, that God will find a way to
bring everyone to heaven in the last day. But in His
justice and fairness He has provided many warnings and
cautions in the Scriptures about the spiritual light and
spiritual responsibilities He has given us. They are directed to us all.

John saw the flashes of lightning. He felt the peals of
rumbling thunder. He heard the mighty voices and the
trumpet blasts as the angels of God held back the soon-
to-be-released judgements coming upon the earth and
the seas. We look around us, and we see this world's cup
of iniquity brim full. One day, when it reaches the point
of overflow, God will say, 'Enough! Open the seals!
Sound the trumpets of judgement!'

The justice of God and the wrath of God have been
ignored and violated so long and so arrogantly that the
day of reckoning must come. The divine lightning, the
peals of thunder and the rumbling of judgement will go
out from the throne.

Some who have misconstrued the meaning of God's
grace will make light of such predictions. But the Bible is
unequivocal: God's throne of grace will become a throne
of judgement.

I confess that I am stirred within my being as I study
these portions of the Revelation. If I were not a Christian, saved and forgiven, I would not wait. I would get
down on my knees and plead for God's grace and mercy
while there is time. I would not deceive my own soul
with the excuse that 'I do not have enough light' or 'I do

not understand all that Christ did' or 'Why am I any worse in God's sight than my neighbour?'

They are only excuses

It is sad but true that many people are going to hell while they try to hide behind a variety of excuses. As a minister, I have never found men and women rejecting the gospel of Christ on the basis of misunderstanding or confusion. Rather, the problem is some dark place in the soul, some secret sin. The rejection of Christ is the refusal to give these things up and come to the light of Christ and follow Him.

I for one never want to be in the tragic condition of living where the light of God cannot reach me. The world of nature has its flatworms and silver-fish and other slimy creepers and crawlers. All of these try desperately to stay out of the light. They can only exist by avoiding the light of the sun. They live under the rocks and in the dark caves and the damp crevices. The last thing they desire is the glorious radiance of the sun. For us, the rays of the sun are part of God's bountiful provision for life and health, but the sun's rays cannot penetrate the hiding places of those creeping, crawling creatures.

I do not want to be like a hidden-away flatworm. I want to live in the light of God's grace and Spirit. Only in that way can I learn more of His love and of His person and character. Though I sense that God has already taught me much, I know there is still much more to be learned. God wants to give me more light, more understanding of His will and His ways. This is a great and far-reaching truth. John expressed it better than I can when he said:

God is light; in him there is no darkness at all. If we claim to
have fellowship with him yet walk in the darkness, we lie
and do not live by the truth. But if we walk in the light, as he
is in the light, we have fellowship with one another, and the
blood of Jesus, his Son, purifies us from every sin.

1 John 1:5–7

A serious-minded young man once talked with me. 'Dr
Tozer,' he said, 'I know that every one of us was brought
into this world with a design for life and for existence.
Why are there so many among us who seem to be drift-
ing, so many with no purpose in life and with no thought
of eternity?'

No person can answer such a searching question for
someone else! But I have analysed it for myself and for
my own life. If I should have missed—rejected—God's
plan of salvation, it would have been far better for me to
have been carried from my mother's arms to the grave
while I was yet an unnamed infant. If I miss this gracious
salvation, I miss the privilege of one day standing around
the throne of God with the redeemed of all ages.

Who is to be blamed?

And if I miss the love and the grace of God in this life,
who is to be blamed? Certainly not the God who sits on
the throne. He made full provision for my salvation.
Certainly not the Lamb who stands before the throne.
He died for my sins and rose again for my justification.
Certainly not the radiant, flaming Holy Spirit who has
accosted men and women all over the world, mediating
to them the saving gospel of Christ.

Hear the words John heard on rocky Patmos as the
Revelation of Jesus Christ concluded:

'Behold, I am coming soon! My reward is with me, and I will give to everyone according to what he has done...

'Blessed are those who wash their robes, that they may have the right to the tree of life and may go through the gates into the city...'

The Spirit and the bride say, 'Come!' And let him who hears say, 'Come!' Whoever is thirsty, let him come; and whoever wishes, let him take the free gift of the water of life.

22:12, 14, 17

If I miss God's great salvation, has this life been worth the struggle? Personally, I think not!

6

The Title Deed—
Worthy Is the Lamb

Then I saw in the right hand of him who sat on the throne a scroll with writing on both sides and sealed with seven seals. And I saw a mighty angel proclaiming in a loud voice, 'Who is worthy to break the seals and open the scroll?' But no-one in heaven or on earth or under the earth could open the scroll or even look inside it. I wept and wept because no-one was found who was worthy to open the scroll or look inside. Then one of the elders said to me, 'Do not weep! See, the Lion of the tribe of Judah, the Root of David, has triumphed. He is able to open the scroll and its seven seals.'

Then I saw a Lamb, looking as if it had been slain, standing in the centre of the throne, encircled by the four living creatures and the elders. He had seven horns and seven eyes, which are the seven spirits of God sent out into all the earth. He came and took the scroll from the right hand of him who sat on the throne. And when he had taken it, the four living creatures and the twenty-four elders fell down before the Lamb. Each one had a harp and they were holding golden bowls full of incense, which are the prayers of the saints....

Then I heard every creature in heaven and on earth and under the earth and on the sea, and all that is in them, singing:

'To him who sits on the throne and to the Lamb be praise and honour and glory and power, for ever and ever!'

Revelation 5:1–8, 13

Have you ever thought about the actual ownership of the planet earth? It has always been a valuable property, and through the centuries individuals and nations have tried to stake out their diverse claims to it. I invite you to spend a little time with me in the fifth chapter of the Revelation as we seek to answer the question, 'Who really owns this world, after all?' and as we consider some implications of that answer.

John is still gazing through the door standing open in heaven. He is being shown important scenes and mighty deeds—cosmic events that will affect the entire created universe.

John sees an important document in the right hand of the one sitting on the throne: a scroll securely sealed with seven seals. Then he hears the voice of a 'mighty angel' asking the entire universe, 'Who is worthy to break the seals and open the scroll?'

Bible commentators have had differing opinions about this written, sealed document. Some have said it might be the Old Testament. Others have countered that it probably was the New Testament. Some scholars have held that it was God's book of judgement. One imaginative person suggested that it was 'the statement of God's hidden purposes'.

A number of other godly students of the word hold

that this scroll was the actual title deed to the created earth. That is what I believe, too, and I think there is scriptural reason for such an opinion.

Our inclination is to say that God owns and controls all things, but Satan and his hosts have long challenged God's right and God's control. Remember the temptation of our Lord and the daring proposition of the devil:

> Again, the devil took him to a very high mountain and showed him all the kingdoms of the world and their splendour. 'All this I will give you,' he said, 'if you will bow down and worship me.'
>
> Jesus said to him, 'Away from me, Satan! For it is written: "Worship the Lord your God, and serve him only".'
>
> *Matthew 4:8–10*

We note that our Lord did not challenge the implied claim Satan made concerning the kingdoms of this world. His reply to the devil was: 'I will not worship you. God alone deserves worship!'

Satan, the usurper

So, Satan has made his claims, and in many ways he has succeeded in exercising control through the centuries, even though he certainly could not produce a title deed.

We need at this point to review the scriptural background of creation and the fall of man. When God created Adam, He said in effect: 'I am giving you the title to this good earth, and I am giving you dominion over it and over the creatures on the earth, the fish in the seas and the birds in the air. There are a few rules you must observe, however. For one, you must not eat of the tree of the knowledge of good and evil!'

Tempted by Satan, Adam and Eve ate the forbidden fruit. Their disobedience introduced death to the human race. The ground was cursed, and sinning mankind forfeited ready fellowship with God. In effect, the Creator God took back the title deed He had given our first parents.

We seldom consider it just this way, but when Adam and Eve succumbed to Satan's proposition in the Garden of Eden, they allowed him to become a squatter—an alien usurper of dominion throughout the earth, even though he did not hold the title deed.

How could the earth ever be redeemed from this encroacher and mankind restored? There was only one way—a seemingly impossible way. There must of necessity be a second Adam. He must be able to meet the tempter and best him. Moreover, because death had come through sin, the second Adam would have to taste death and emerge its victor. Only in such a way could mankind win back all that had been lost in the Garden.

Who does this world belong to?

Who owns the world? Ever since God's right to His creation has been challenged by the forces of Satan and the fantasies of sinful men and women, our world has had its succession of dark and dreadful rulers.

The intellectuals—those wise in this world's wisdom—would have us believe that only they have the capacity for dominance and rulership. It is just as well that they have not usually prevailed. It would be grim, indeed, if the course of this world were shaped by the thinkers. Most of them seem miserable and unhappy. Ecclesiastes is the soliloquy of perhaps the world's wisest man—a great thinker. He becomes more gloomy as he goes along. Finally, after 'devot[ing] [him]self to study and to explore by wisdom all that is done under heaven' (Ecclesiastes 1:13), he comes to this morbid exclamation:

> 'Meaningless! Meaningless!' says the Teacher, 'Everything is meaningless!'
>
> *Ecclesiastes 12:8*

Another group who insist they are capable of wielding world power are the blue-collar workers—those who toil for a living. Their slogan has been a popular one in this century: 'Workers of the world, arise! You have nothing to lose but your chains!' But we have discovered to our sorrow that worker power is no better than the moral level of the workers; once in authority, they can be both cruel and tyrannical.

Probably I should also mention the scientists in this discussion of world force and technology. Some think the scientists are qualified to exercise world oversight. But what do we see? On the one hand, we see learned men and women able to heal and save lives. On the other hand, we see men and women inventing new ways to destroy the greatest number of people in the shortest space of time. The scientists have not demonstrated their ability to bring good government to our world.

Then, there are the claims of the various human races. From the Pharaohs of ancient Egypt to the cataclysmic, racial-inspired wars of this century, we have seen the devastation heaped upon mankind as one or another race sought to assert its superiority.

When Jesus Christ was on earth, He warned His followers in plain language that wars and rumours of war would continue right up to the time of His return. We are reluctant witnesses to the truth of His words. In the dark days of the Second World War, when the outcome of that conflagration was still in the balance, this was my Christian counsel to my congregation:

'No matter how things look to us now, sin and murder and violence cannot win at last. Righteousness and godliness cannot fail at last. Prophecy must be fulfilled. We will see the day when Germany's mouthing maniac will go down like a rotten tree felled on the hillside. Let us stay by our faith. It is still right to be good, and it is still wrong to follow evil. God must still rule His world, and Christ must still be the acclaimed King throughout the universe.' I believed it then. I believe it yet.

Communism is no different

Since those days, Communism has reared its head. Millions have feared that it was only a matter of time until the world would be under Communist ideology and control. Silly, frightened people declared they would 'rather be Red than dead'. But communism cannot prevail, and I will tell you why. It has nothing to do with politics or economics or public ownership of property.

Communism cannot prevail because it begins with materialism. It teaches that there is no God and no Christ, no heaven and no hell. It declares that mankind has no soul and that prayer to God is nonsense. Communism is a negation of everything good and pure, everything divine and holy. It cannot prevail because our God in heaven has His plan and programme for creation. There is no human being and no human philosophy or force able to wrest dominion from our living God.

When John looked through the open door into heaven, he saw this significant title deed in the hands of God, who sat on the throne. The great angel's voice went throughout creation as if in challenge to Satan and every created being: 'Who is worthy to break the seals and open the scroll?'

And what was the response? *No one* in heaven or on earth or under the earth was qualified to open the scroll or to look inside it. All of this uncertainty was too much for the sensitive, tender John. I have often thought of John's great heart of love and concern and have decided that I would rather have a heart like his than all the knowledge this world holds.

We must not forget that John was still human and still much a part of the earth scene when he received this vision. He was not yet glorified, not yet perfected. In his own being, John treasured the prospect of God's control and ownership of our lost planet. John knew from observation and experience the tell-tale signs of having the wrong person in political charge. He was isolated on Patmos because of his Christian testimony.

I think John carried the grief of the human race in his heart. That was why God chose him to receive the Revelation. God always blesses the men and women who have concern enough in their hearts to bring tears of love and compassion to their eyes. We have many ways of teaching the Bible and theology—and I believe in them. But I must insist that the Spirit of God will reveal some of the secrets of God only to those who know what it means to have a broken heart for Jesus' sake and on behalf of lost humanity.

So, one of the elders said to John, 'Do not weep! See, the Lion of the tribe of Judah, the Root of David, has triumphed. He is able to open the scroll and its seven seals.' John knew what a lion was like, and he turned in expectation. But the one he saw was not a lion but a Lamb—the Lamb of God!

Then I saw a Lamb, looking as if it had been slain, standing in the centre of the throne, encircled by the four living creatures and the elders....He came and took the scroll from the right hand of him who sat on the throne....

Then I heard every creature in heaven and on earth and under the earth and on the sea, and all that is in them, singing:

'To him who sits on the throne and to the Lamb be praise and honour and glory and power, for ever and ever!'

5:6–7, 13

Now, I want to look back with you to this scene in which the Lion and the Lamb are mentioned. The association seems odd to us. We wonder how it could be. John was told that the Lion of the tribe of Judah was the conqueror, but when he turned, he saw not the fearful and powerful Lion but the wondrous Lamb of God, the risen and eternal Christ.

Let us fully understand this truth. On earth, the lion is stronger than the lamb. But in the kingdom of God and before the throne of God, the Lamb is stronger, and He is victor! God's ways and ours are not the same. When John turned, he saw Christ, the Lion, but in truth he saw Him as the Lamb. Unless we know Jesus Christ as both Lamb, our Redeemer, and Lion, our strength to live for Him day by day, we are not Christians in the right sense of the word. In the kingdoms of earth, the spirit of the lion dominates; in the kingdom of God, the Lamb rules. For this reason the world's redemption is not in mankind's hands.

If you get nothing else from this chapter, it is essential that you understand and retain this truth: *the world's redemption is not in mankind's hands*. I cannot tell you how glad I am that there is at least one thing that we humans cannot bungle. The plan of salvation is God's plan. The power in redemption is God's power. Only the Lamb of God could die in our place. This is God's way of doing things, not ours.

Not the strong fists, but the nail-pierced hands

God redeemed lost mankind not by the strong fists of Jesus but by His nail-pierced hands. We do not sing about the power of the clenched fist; we sing with thanksgiving that we 'shall know Him by the print of the nails in His hands'. This gospel of Jesus Christ is unique. There is nothing within it that brings glory or credit to our human means or methods. Our redemption was not by muscle, but by love. It was not wrought by vengeance, but by forgiveness. It was not by sword, but by sacrifice.

We are Christians because Jesus destroyed His enemies by dying for them. He conquered death by letting death conquer Him, and then He turned death inside out as He burst forth from the tomb as victor! This whole work of redemption had to be accomplished in the way things are done in heaven. That is why I say that as Christians, we have learned that whatever Christ the Lion will do in bringing the world into submission, He will do because of what He has already done as the Lamb of God.

The scenes in this part of the Revelation are not provincial. By that, I mean they do not deal just with Israel or just with the church. If you please, they do not even deal just with our planet. Almighty God is dealing with all of His vast, created universe. The unlimited search for one worthy to claim the title deed to creation was indeed a universal search. Not just earth, but our whole universe awaits the consummation. Who is worthy? Who is able? Who is the Conqueror?

In this world, ruined and turned upside down by sin, God has a better way, whether or not people will accept it. Jesus invaded our world as God's Christ. He conquered by the shedding of His own blood. For the first and only time, victory was fashioned in such an unorthodox way. Now the Lamb, who is also the Lion, stands in the midst of that heavenly throne.

God is saying to all the universe: 'The time has come for you to understand that I am God. Earthlings must give up their sinful, distorted ideas of strength and power and dominion. Only this victorious Lamb is worthy to claim the title deed to the created universe and to open the seals that are holding back My judgements.'

Not a pleasant subject

Judgement and God's wrath are not pleasant subjects. I know people who turn away, saying with finality: 'I do not even want to think about judgement. I will not discuss it!'

We do not fully understand all of God's purposes in preserving for our time and generation this Revelation. But we do know that this world's cup of iniquity is filling up. We know there are warnings in this book that continually urge us to be watchful, thoughtful believers.

I am convinced of this: we Christians in our minds and hearts must always be correcting what we hear and see against the truth of heaven. Otherwise, we will be carried away by the world and its distorted human ways and values. How did the nations of earth come to be what they are? By tooth and claw—the law of the jungle. The questions of justice, right and righteousness—these scarcely come up at all. I confess that I am afraid for this sinful and violent society. I am afraid, indeed, for the millions and millions of men and women who defy God, who hate Jesus Christ and who are willing dupes of Satan.

When the cup of iniquity is full, God cannot withhold judgement any longer. The Bible gives us an ample, frightening preview of the tribulation that will come upon the earth. In our Christian circles the question often is asked, 'Will the church go through the tribulation? Will the church be raptured out of this world before the great tribulation begins?'

There are differences of opinion and a variety of interpretations concerning the sequence of events when Christ returns. I am not among those who claim to have all the answers. I know there is a time of great tribulation coming upon our world. Whether the church of Jesus Christ shall escape all of that judgement and suffering is not clear. I *fear* the church will suffer trial and tribulation. At the same time, I have a great *hope* that it will not!

I shall not argue about it. I will not debate the matter. For myself, I know I do not want to be on this earth when that worst of all times comes—when God rises up and shakes the earth and the nations so that those things that cannot be shaken may remain.

John has described the heavenly scene in which the angels of God are being prepared for the judgements that must come upon this planet. I can only wonder how much longer the holy patience of God can stand by in grace and mercy.

The Lamb of God is the Conqueror. John saw that confirmed at the throne of God in heaven. The day may be near when the Conqueror goes forth to establish His righteous rule in all the earth!

7

The Beginning of Judgements— The Four Horsemen

I watched as the Lamb opened the first of the seven seals. Then I heard one of the four living creatures say in a voice like thunder, 'Come!' I looked, and there before me was a white horse! Its rider held a bow, and he was given a crown, and he rode out as a conqueror bent on conquest.

When the Lamb opened the second seal, I heard the second living creature say, 'Come!' Then another horse came out, a fiery red one. Its rider was given power to take peace from the earth and to make men slay each other. To him was given a large sword.

When the Lamb opened the third seal, I heard the third living creature say, 'Come!' I looked, and there before me was a black horse! Its rider was holding a pair of scales in his hand. Then I heard what sounded like a voice among the four living creatures, saying, 'A quart of wheat for a day's wages, and three quarts of barley for a day's wages, and do not damage the oil and the wine!'

When the Lamb opened the fourth seal, I heard the voice of the fourth living creature say, 'Come!' I

*looked, and there before me was a pale horse! Its
rider was named Death, and Hades was following
close behind him. They were given power over a
fourth of the earth to kill by sword, famine and
plague, and by the wild beasts of the earth....*

*Then the kings of the earth, the princes, the gen-
erals, the rich, the mighty, and every slave and every
free man hid in caves and among the rocks of the
mountains. They called to the mountains and the
rocks, 'Fall on us and hide us from the face of him
who sits on the throne and from the wrath of the
Lamb! For the great day of their wrath has come,
and who can stand?'*

Revelation 6:1–8, 15–17

In all of secular and sacred literature, perhaps no other
cast of characters has evoked the kind of universal discussion and conjecture accorded the four horsemen of
the Apocalypse. Because the Scriptures present the dramatic appearances of these four horsemen against the
vivid backdrop of God's wrath and judgement, most
humans have ultimately reacted with incredulity:

'The judgements cannot be real. The famine, the
plagues cannot be real. Our world is too good; men and
women are too good to deserve the judgement of God.
Forget the whole idea. Think nothing more about it.
Such a judgement will never happen.'

Even in the worst of its dark and fearsome times, the
human race has never given up hoping for 'something
better' to happen in the future. The poet sensed that
yearning when he pointed out the often quoted truth:
'Hope springs eternal in the human breast.'

Men and women have never given up their fond hope
that the earth next year—or perhaps the year after

that—will be a better place in which to live! In spite of war and rumours of war, men and women never abandon their unfounded hope that lasting peace is about to become reality.

Politicians have learned that they can garner votes if they will fan the hopes of constituents that this world actually can be made a place of universal health. I listen to the campaign speeches of the candidates for public office. Their appeal is based largely on their promise to solve all economic and social problems. Then, after four years, we discover that our 'paradise' has not happened.

Even in the realm of the church and religion, we hear expressions of hope that religious unity can be achieved. These churchmen fondly hope that the social problems will go away once everyone is worshipping in one large church. The extra and unnecessary church properties can become playgrounds and recreational centres for the well-being of the deprived children in our communities.

A sharp contrast

I have cited these often expressed hopes because they are in sharp contrast to what we see concerning the four horsemen of the Revelation. In doing so, I abandon any lingering hope of popularity, for what I see is counter to our natural desires for peace, tranquillity and unity. But I am committed to the truth, whether or not it is popular. And the truth is that all of these human hopes we have reviewed are vain hopes. This world is not going to get better under human government.

Likely you know someone who is terminally ill. If you learn of even slight improvement in the person's condition, you are glad. But in your heart of hearts you know the change is temporary. Death is only a matter of time.

In the case of our world, it received a mortal wound some six millenniums ago. A preacher here and there may say, 'I think I see a little improvement.' But this is a sinful and rebellious world. Its long list of ailments and ills will not fade away. The longer-term prognosis has not changed. The world is not going to heal itself.

In this section of the Revelation there is a noticeable sense of heavenly excitement. There is intense interest, eager expectation and ecstatic worship as the Lion of the tribe of Judah steps forward. The one who has conquered as the Lamb of God steps forward to receive the seven-sealed scroll, a written document that is best understood as the accredited title deed to this earth.

There is a burst of acclamation around the heavenly throne as every voice sings:

> Worthy is the Lamb, who was slain, to receive power and wealth and wisdom and strength and honour and glory and praise!
>
> *5:12*

Then John heard the most unusual sound of all: the voices of 'every creature in heaven and on earth and under the earth and on the sea...singing, "To him who sits on the throne and to the Lamb be praise and honour and glory and power, for ever and ever!" ' (5:13).

And he adds, 'The four living creatures said, "Amen," and the elders fell down and worshipped.'

The mysterious seals

The sixth chapter begins abruptly with the opening of the mysterious seals having to do with the title deed to this earth. John tells us he watched as the Lamb opened the first of the seven seals. At once, one of the living creatures said in a voice like thunder, 'Come!' This is the long-awaited signal to the four horsemen that the hour has come for them to gallop forth on their missions of judgement.

When Jesus was on earth two thousand years ago, He told His hearers that the 'day of the Lord' was coming. He said no one except the Father in heaven knew the day or the hour. It is our understanding that God's patience and His time of grace will endure until the world's cup of iniquity overflows. According to the Scriptures, patience—the ability to wait—is one of the fruits of the Holy Spirit. The human, natural part of us does not like to wait for anything. But the great God Almighty, who has all of eternity to accomplish His purposes, can afford to wait. In our creature impatience we are prone to cry out, 'Oh God, how long? How long?' And God replies, in effect, 'Why are you in such a hurry? We have an eternity stretching before us. Why get excited and irritated?'

Apparently the four symbolic steeds have been prepared and waiting for this summons. In equestrian language, they were 'champing at the bit'. But they had to wait for events on earth and in heaven to run their course before they could go into action. During that long wait, generations of Christian believers have lived with the expectation of the Lord's return to earth. Not all of them were patient. Not all of them had the ability to wait. Some began to say, 'He will not return!'

Now, John continues with the narration of what he saw:

I looked, and there before me was a white horse! Its rider

held a bow, and he was given a crown, and he rode out as a conqueror bent on conquest.

Some have asked, 'Could this rider on the white horse be Christ Jesus?' The answer is a definite 'No'. Within this context, he could not possibly be Christ Jesus, for it is Christ Jesus—the Lamb—who has broken the seal that frees the horseman to go forth. Inasmuch as all four of these horsemen are connected with judgement, we must identify the rider of the white horse as one who will prove to be a deceiver of mankind and a curse. Most scholars, indeed, look upon him as the antichrist.

An antichrist will come

In other places in the Bible such an antichrist is announced (see, for example, 1 John 4:3). Destined to appear at some future time of world crisis, he will be a deceiver, conquering by lies and duplicity (see Daniel 8:23–25). He will be known as 'the man of lawlessness' (2 Thessalonians 2:3), and in the course of his dominance over mankind he will ultimately exalt himself as God.

There is reason to expect that those who are pressing for one great world church will welcome and co-operate with the antichrist when he appears. Indeed, he will be favourable to religious interests—for a while! When he sees the church wishing to move in a certain direction, he will say to the membership, 'The key to this objective is to be tolerant—you must love everybody!' Then, while men and women are busy loving everybody and being tolerant, those religious leaders will take over and put their stamp upon the world.

We have had illustrations of this in our own time.

While men and women are intent on brotherhood, love and unity, teachers are busy telling our young people in high school and college that God did not create the heavens and the earth, that Adam and Eve did not really exist, that Christ's resurrection from the dead is a myth.

Yes, an antichrist is destined to enter the world scene. His control, as I said, will be through duplicity and delusion. He will appear to be an amiable person, able to head up and harness all the divergent political, economic and religious forces. Ultimately he will turn out to be the embodiment of everything that is contrary to our Lord Jesus Christ. When he comes, he will talk much about peace and prosperity. But during his regime, war will come. That armed conflict is the signal for the second horse to appear.

The fiery red horse of war

This second horseman 'was given power to take peace from the earth and to make men slay each other'. The pacifists and the optimists will argue against this portrait of future war. But the antichrist's campaign of religious brotherhood and international peace will be short-lived. Satan is the world's greatest counterfeiter, and he is behind the duplicity of this counterfeit Christ!

Suppose some person or force in our world could proclaim that tomorrow morning all wars and all conflict would cease, that all soldiers, sailors and airmen would go home, that all military bases would be permanently closed, that the entrenched military industrial complex would be no more. The proclamation would call for complete world disarmament; no nation would be permitted to go to war ever again.

What would follow in the wake of such a world-wide

edict? Everyone knows the answer. The worst economic
depression in the history of mankind would quickly
develop. Where would the world's governments find
jobs for the millions of people who are currently a part of
the defence and military establishments? Or for the
added millions whose jobs are in the civilian support
networks for the nations' armies?

The antichrist has promised prosperity. To achieve it,
he will resort to war and conquest. John was told that
this second horseman was given power to take peace
from the world and 'to make men slay each other'. When
this horseman rides forth, any temporary treaties of
peace and co-operation will be disregarded. We are
reminded of what the apostle Paul predicted would happen as the 'day of the Lord' came: 'While people are
saying, "Peace and safety", destruction will come on
them suddenly, as labour pains on a pregnant woman,
and they will not escape' (1 Thessalonians 5:3). The
symbolism is plain. This rider with the character of war
has a great sword given to him—a sword that surely
represents mankind's capacity to wage international warfare.

Aftermath of war: famine and death

When the third living creature issues his thunderous
invitation to 'Come!' a black horse charges into the
world arena. The description of the rider of the black
horse is clearly famine.

It should not be surprising to us that famine and
hunger will follow quickly on the heels of war and the
disdain for human life. We have seen it happen too many
times. When vast sections of humanity are affected by
war, the dislocated masses begin to starve.

Inevitably, the fourth horseman rides abroad on his pale steed. There is no mistaking his identity. Death is his name. John records that the forces of Hades—hell—come along closely behind him. To the power of death by sword is added the power of death by famine, plague and wild beast.

We really have no idea what world conditions will be in that day. Biological warfare will be added to the destructive elements already in use. Plague is the name for it: diseases that quickly break forth from the rotting corpses that no one has time to mourn or to bury. And when these four seals have been broken by the victorious Lamb, judgement and tribulation, pain and death will overflow our earth.

You may be accusing me of extreme pessimism. So be it. But I must agree with what John foretells, for it is a part of the Bible, and the Bible is wholly true. We live in the midst of an ungodly society—a world that rebels against our God and His Christ. I do not find anything in the word of God to encourage this generation in its present godless life-style. It resolves no problems for men and women to say to each other, 'Cheer up! Things will get better!' All is *not* well. Things will *not* get better while the horses of the apocalypse are pawing the ground and champing at the bit, awaiting the signal to gallop forth.

As I close this chapter, I want to tie in the loosing of these four horsemen with John's vision of the souls of the martyrs beneath the altar (6:9–11) when the fifth seal is broken. John says he immediately heard the 'loud... call' of these souls 'under the altar'. Their appeal: 'How long, Sovereign Lord, holy and true, until you judge the inhabitants of the earth and avenge our blood?'

I think it is beautiful how God answers them as a mother might comfort her children. John says, 'Then

each of them was given a white robe, and they were told
to wait a little longer, until the number of their fellow-
servants and brothers who were to be killed as they had
been, was completed.' It is as if God says, 'Hush, My
dear children. Do not be impatient. We are waiting a
little longer until the souls of the other faithful martyrs
are gathered in. They are giving up their lives even as
you have given yours. Meanwhile, here are shining robes
to wear until the time is ripe!'

The martyrs' place

I doubt that the souls of these martyrs are in some
segregated part of the heavenly realm. John hears their
appeal at this time because of the judgements about to
take place. Further, I do not interpret their call as blood-
thirsty. My mind goes out to the great roll call of the
faithful, holy men and women slain in every century for
their testimony of love for Jesus Christ. I think, for
example, of Stephen, stoned to death by infuriated Jews
whom he had charged with the betrayal and murder of
God's righteous one. But as he died, Stephen prayed,
'Lord, do not hold this sin against them' (Acts 7:60).

The breaking of that fifth seal seems to indicate that
the martyrs had never been told earlier that God would
never forget their love, loyalty and obedience to Jesus
Christ. Vengeance, the Bible admonishes us, does not
belong to us (Romans 12:19). As Christians, we willingly
live for God in a hostile world because God has already
whispered to us, 'Be patient; be kind! Any vengeance
that is necessary will be My holy vengeance. I will repay!'

Surely we do not think often enough of this great
company of overcomers who have told their tormentors
on this earth: 'Do what you want with us. We will love

and honour our Saviour, Jesus Christ—to the death if necessary!' When our godless society martyrs a saint of God, it is a frightful act of injustice—an unspeakable act of fallen man's deepest depravity.

History has a way of mixing up the accounts and colouring the tales men tell, but God in heaven keeps faithful records. He alone knows every detail about the faith and courage of every person who has laid down his or her human life for the Saviour, Jesus Christ. So this cry as the martyrs wait is not a cry for blood. It is a cry for the day and hour when God's judgement upon all of mankind's sin and unholiness will come.

We are right in believing that God has a plan and that it is both fixed and eternal. I do not dismiss the Revelation. I do not dismiss the fact that God is going to deal with Satan—that deadly, cunning usurper of God's created earth. I do not try to explain away these coming judgements. I trust the prediction of the Scriptures that these four horsemen of judgement and death will ride out over the nations of this earth. I take this view because I know that men and women once created in the image of God, now continue to violate His holy laws, hour after hour, year after year.

One of my burdens

I share with you one of my great burdens concerning our present generation. Our wisest and most brilliant people have played with the secrets of God Almighty, the Creator. I do not know how we can justify it. For the first time in the history of the world, we have released the secret of the composition of matter. Sinful men have entered into that holy place where life begins. We have

glorified our test tubes, our microscopes, our instruments of technology, prying into the secrets of creation
and life—secrets that have always belonged only to God.

The problems of death and destruction we have not
solved. Nuclear destruction is out of the bottle—and
becoming more menacing by the year. The common
people do not really know the extent to which their
leaders have mortgaged their futures. So they repress
their fears and doubts by seeking pleasure and living
selfishly, intent only on themselves. Someone has
described their life-style as 'pampered opulence'. While
the world is falling apart, they are spending billions on
fun and on pleasure and on what they call excitement.

We may have differing opinions about the symbols
and details of prophetic warnings, but God's truth is
here. We cannot get around it. Into history, into our
world, the horsemen of the Apocalypse will come riding
forth in God's time. Dare we imagine we can live in
pampered opulence—not even remembering to pray for
this dying world—and still believe we will be ready for
that hour when our Lord will call His people home?

As a minister of God's word, I add my caution to
every caution and warning God has given us. If we are
wasting our time and money and energy in foolish play,
it will be tragic for us in that awful, coming hour.

I pray for myself. I pray that I may be more detached
from this world and from its evils and its selfish systems.
I pray that I may recognise that soft, silky, deceptive
voice that is opposed to our Lord Jesus Christ. I pray
that I will be able to stand with the overcomers, even if it
means that everyone around me is as enemy, even if it
means martyrdom.

Do you feel that way about these important issues? I
hope you do!

8

The Overcomers— Out of the Great Tribulation

After this I saw four angels standing at the four corners of the earth, holding back the four winds of the earth to prevent any wind from blowing on the land or on the sea or on any tree. Then I saw another angel coming up from the east, having the seal of the living God. He called out in a loud voice to the four angels who had been given power to harm the land and the sea.... Then I heard the number of those who were sealed: 144,000 from all the tribes of Israel....

After this I looked and there before me was a great multitude that no-one could count, from every nation, tribe, people and language, standing before the throne and in front of the Lamb. They were wearing white robes and were holding palm branches in their hands....

Then one of the elders asked me, 'These in white robes—who are they, and where did they come from?'

I answered, 'Sir, you know.'

And he said, 'These are they who have come out of the great tribulation; they have washed their robes

and made them white in the blood of the Lamb.'
Revelation 7:1–4, 9, 13–14

The most tragic and unavailing prayer meeting in the history of the world is described for us in the sixth chapter of the Revelation. In the seventh, the apostle John reports the greatest ever assembly of the redeemed for praise and worship. Both events follow the unloosing in heaven of the mysterious sixth seal by the worthy, victorious Lamb of God.

All varieties of prayer—cries and groans, shouts and demands, moans and whispers—will be heard in that coming day of the Lord when the forces of judgement are released, when the stars begin to fall, when even the mountains and the islands will be removed from their places. But by then the prayers and cries of sinful men and women will be too little and too late. All of the great men of the earth, all of the important people, all who have mistakenly put their trust and their hope in purely human abilities will join those crying out in guilt. They will call on the crumbling rocks and mountains to fall on them to hide them from the wrath of God.

John foresees a great earthquake. The sun turns black. The moon becomes blood-red. Stars fall to the earth. The sky recedes like a scroll and every mountain and island is dislocated.

I am among those who believe that the judgements of God are certain. God is indeed going to shake the earth as it has never been shaken before. I do not know the day when these events will happen. I do not know the hour. That is confidential information known only to my heavenly Father. Jesus himself told us not to waste our efforts speculating on 'the times and dates the Father has set by his own authority' (Acts 1:7).

As these seals are opened, our earth experiences heavenly phenomena that rock and shake the planet. The earthquake that will take place will be devastating in its destruction.

I have never experienced an earthquake. Those who have say the greatest terror is the sudden and extreme loss of confidence in the earth itself. Psychologists confirm that such an experience can leave the human system in deep, long-term shock. Until the moment of the quake, the earth has been a stable, supportive friend. Suddenly it is that no longer! Floors, walls, ceilings are no longer fixed and certain. Everything—including the earth itself—seems to recede. The shaking, the rocking, the rumbling—all of these phenomena tell the finite human being that his or her life-long confidence in the *terra firma* has been a misplaced trust.

Far beyond man's tinkering

We have become complacent about scientific technology and space exploration. We even joke about all the American and Russian metal orbiting the earth and speculate that some sort of a space traffic cop will soon be necessary to keep the traffic lanes open!

But these things that mankind and nations do as a result of their science and technology are as nothing compared with the shaking that will occur after the opening of the sixth seal. At least up until this time, our discoveries and experiments in space have not affected the sun and the stars. But God intends to take things out of human hands and human control. In an instant he will convince mankind and nations of the fatal mistake they have made—the mistake of forgetting God and elevating human ability and performance in the place of God.

What God has to say to us in Revelation 6 is a sobering preview. Even for us who are Christians it is difficult to realise the extent of this divine judgement upon our earth. In a word, *all* inhabitants left on the earth—'kings of the earth, the princes, the generals, the rich, the mighty, and every slave and every free man'—will be reduced to helplessness and stark fear. Regardless of status, rank or position, men and women will seek a hiding place from God's wrath: 'They called to the mountains and the rocks, "Fall on us and hide us from the face of him who sits on the throne and from the wrath of the Lamb! For the great day of their wrath has come, and who can stand?"'

God is obliged to bring this event to pass. Proud and sinful humans, in their blasphemous pursuits, have long profaned the name of Jesus, the heavenly Lamb. They have imagined themselves smart enough, able enough, strong enough to be successful in their rebellion against the suffering Saviour.

The outraged Lamb

People might have imagined that the *Lion* of Judah had a measure of power and strength. But suddenly God reveals His wrath through the outraged *Lamb*. It is the Lamb who has been found worthy! It is the Lamb who is the Victor, the Overcomer! It is the Lamb of God, God's eternal Son, into whose hands the Father has committed all justice and judgement!

What a great responsibility God has laid upon us preachers of His gospel and teachers of His word. In that future day when God's wrath is poured out, how are we going to answer? How am *I* going to answer? I fear there is much we are doing in the name of the Christian church that is wood, hay and stubble destined to be burned up in God's refining fire. A day is coming when I and my fellow ministers must give account of our stewardship:

What kind of a gospel did we preach?

Did we make it plain that men and women who are apart from Christ Jesus are lost?

Did we counsel them to repent and believe?

Did we tell them of the regenerating power of the Holy Spirit?

Did we warn them of the wrath of the Lamb—the crucified, resurrected, outraged Lamb of God?

With that kind of accounting yet to come, the question John hears from the human objects of God's wrath is especially significant: 'Who can stand?' (6:17). Who indeed?

I reflect back to the evangelistic preaching throughout the cities of America by the famous Billy Sunday. Billy Sunday had many critics, but he ploughed a deep furrow for God in the hearts and minds of sinful, lost men and women. In his meetings, Billy frequently used a song entitled, 'The Great Judgement Morning'. We no longer hear it in our churches, and that does not speak well for our theology. Perhaps we have gone soft on judgement and accountability. Perhaps we have gone soft on our responsibility to the lost.

But Billy Sunday told people they were destined to face the judgement of God. 'The Great Judgement Morning' sung in his meetings told of one person's dream of judgement morning when the great man's greatness was no more and the rich man's wealth had disappeared. All that remained was the haunting question, 'Who shall be able to stand?'

I thank God that there is an answer to that question. Those who have quit their sin, who are clothed in Jesus

Christ's righteousness—they will be able to stand! The reason the kings and the great men, the slaves and the free men are in such terror is because they love their sin more than anything else. Sin is just too dear to give up.

What price earth's baubles?

I heard of a Kansas farm family endangered by a sudden, descending tornado. The mother quickly herded all her children into the safety of a storm cellar below ground level. But then, in a moment, she disappeared—dashing up into the house to save a little knick-knack that she treasured for sentimental value. Before she could return to safety, that roaring, twisting funnel of wind and fury tore the house to pieces. In minutes it passed and was gone. The children found their mother in the rubble— bleeding, unconscious and dying.

Who will be able to stand? Those who have given up their worthless earthly trinkets, those who have quit loving this world above all else, those who have abandoned hope that anything down here is of permanence and value, those who have come to hate their own sin as God hates it—*they* will be able to stand!

The Revelation refers often to the overcomers in that future day. They will be able to stand then because they have stood firm here and now against every effort of the devil to discourage and tempt and deceive them.

The scene changes

We leave the scene of earthly judgement as we move into chapter 7 of the Revelation. There John describes a scene of joyful praise and worship unmatched in all of history. John sees 'a great multitude that no-one could count, from every nation, tribe, people and language, standing before the throne and in front of the Lamb'. John goes on to say, 'They were wearing white robes and were holding palm branches in their hands'. And their song was an anthem of praise to God and the Lamb:

> Amen!
> Praise and glory
> and wisdom and thanks and honour
> and power and strength
> be to our God for ever and ever.
> Amen!

While God's judgements are visited upon the earth, the overcomers seem to be spared to join the vast throng of the redeemed and glorified saints in heaven.

The chapter begins with an amazing description of four strong angels holding back the four winds of the earth—winds of judgement and distress. As they wait, another angel calls out to them, 'Do not harm the land or the sea or the trees until we put a seal on the foreheads of the servants of our God' (7:3).

The seal was used in the Old Testament

God's use of a seal on His faithful people is not unprecedented. In Ezekiel 9, God instructed the 'man clothed in linen' to 'go throughout the city of Jerusalem and put a mark on the foreheads of those who grieve and lament over all the detestable things that are done in it' (9:4). Then, to the six men with the 'deadly weapons' God commands: 'Follow him through the city and kill, without showing pity or compassion. Slaughter old men, young men and maidens, women and children, but do not touch anyone who has the mark. Begin at my sanctuary' (9:5–6). Ezekiel adds, 'So they began with the elders who were in front of the temple'.

Next John describes God's sealing of the 144,000 'from all the tribes of Israel', twelve thousand from each of the twelve tribes (7:4–8). I do not in the least agree with the numerous cults and far-out religious groups who insist that only they themselves will be sealed as God's elect. Many of us in the evangelical tradition are convinced the Bible predicts a glorious, eternal future for a believing 'remnant' within Jewry. How does the present state of Israel fit into the picture? With all my heart I believe that God did not lie to Abraham! There will be a remnant of believing Jews, restored from north, south, east and west, who will occupy the land God gave to Abraham, Isaac and Jacob.

But I press on now to John's portrayal of the great host of redeemed saints praising and worshipping God around the heavenly throne. This is certainly one of the most amazing passages in the entire Bible—and, in my opinion, one of the most beautiful.

John succeeds as well as anyone could in describing the great multitude from every tribe and nation and language on earth. All are clothed in white robes. All hold palm branches signifying victory. And they are crying out:

> Salvation belongs to our God,
> who sits on the throne,
> and to the Lamb.

Then they join the host of angels around the throne, together with the elders and the living creatures in a song of praise and adoration:

Amen
Praise and glory
and wisdom and thanks and honour
and power and strength
be to our God for ever and ever.
Amen!

I have tried to think what my own emotions and delight would be if I, like John, could have been a witness to this heavenly outpouring of worship and praise. John must have been ecstatic. He must have been speechless with reverence and awe.

John is asked a question

Suddenly, one of the heavenly elders asked John a question. 'These in white robes—who are they, and where did they come from?' John was an example of true Christian humility. This apostle who had spent three years in the company of Jesus, who had devoted a lifetime to teaching and pastoral ministry, did not fish around for some expansive answer that would reveal his expertise and knowledge. He simply shook his head and replied, 'Sir, you know.' This was the true John. How I would like to say to him, 'John, what a wonderful and humble Christian brother you are! How I would like to be more like you!'

So the elder tells John:

These are they who have come out of the great tribulation; they have washed their robes and made them white in the blood of the Lamb. Therefore, they are before the throne of God and serve him day and night in his temple; and he who sits on the throne will spread his tent over them. Never again will they hunger; never again will they thirst. The sun will not beat upon them, nor any scorching heat. For the Lamb at the centre of the throne will be their shepherd; he will lead them to springs of living water. And God will wipe away every tear from their eyes.

Where in all this world could we turn to find anything as beautiful, as powerful, as overwhelming as this description of the overcoming saints of God in heaven? I recommend that we stop reading the shallow, worldly stuff of our day—material that is not doing our souls any good. We should concentrate more of our time and attention on where we are going for eternity.

The assembly of saints described in this chapter of the Revelation is a specific company. I know that. But all of these things that God is doing for them, He has promised to do for all of His believing children. We should not be engaged in useless argument about who may be called upon to suffer and even give their lives for the testimony of Jesus Christ. Concerning this numberless multitude John is told that they have come through the great tribulation. On earth their witness and stand for Christ cost them everything, but in heaven they are the overcomers around the royal throne.

We are twentieth century Christians. Some of us are Christians only because it is convenient and pleasant and because it is not costing us anything. But here is the truth, whether we like it or not: the average evangelical Christian who claims to be born again and have eternal life is not doing as much to propagate his or her faith as the busy adherents of the cults handing out their papers on the street corners and visiting from house to house.

We are not willing to take the spit and the contempt and the abuses those cultists take as they knock on doors and try to persuade everyone to follow them in their mistaken beliefs. The cultists can teach us much about zeal and effort and sacrifice, but most of us do not want to get that serious about our faith—or our Saviour.

Please do not misunderstand. Salvation and heaven are by God's grace and mercy, both unmerited, and not by our works. If we are in the kingdom of God, it is only by the blood of the Lamb. His death and resurrection justified us; His Spirit brought us to life. But we also know the nature of this world in which we are supposed to be living for Christ. If we are serious about our Christian witness, the day may be near when we may be persecuted—even killed—for our faith. We should be stirred, as John was stirred, as we witness this vast company of God's saints in heaven who have come through earth's great tribulation.

I am not saying we are not Christians. I am only trying to find out why we are so far from revival and refreshing and renewal. I am only trying to determine why we are so far from recognising the urgency of God's will laid upon us by the Holy Spirit.

We must not be afraid of the cost

If we belong to Jesus Christ, we should never compromise our spiritual decisions on the basis of 'What is this going to cost me?' We ought only to ask, 'What is my spiritual duty and my spiritual privilege before God?'

I thank God for John's vision of a company of believers so large that the number could not be calculated. The bodies of many of them had been burned at the stake. They had been tossed to the lions. They had undergone slow, agonising torture. They could have collaborated with the enemy of their souls. They could have compromised for the sake of expediency and comfort. Instead, they faced the firing squads, the torture, the many cruel instruments of death, the terror of pain and suffering—for Jesus' sake! 'Therefore they are before the throne of God' (7:15). 'They have washed their robes and made them white in the blood of the Lamb' (7:14).

There is no limit to what God could do in our world if we would dare to surrender before Him with a commitment like this:

> Oh God, I hereby give myself to You. I give my family. I give my business. I give all I possess. Take all of it, Lord— and take me! I give myself in such measure that if it is necessary that I lose everything for your sake, let me lose it. I will not ask what the price is. I will ask only that I may be all that I ought to be as a follower and disciple of Jesus Christ, my Lord. Amen.

If even three hundred of God's people became that serious, our world would never hear the last of it! They would influence the news. Their message would go everywhere like birds on the wing. They would set off a great revival of New Testament faith and witness.

God wants to deliver us from the easy-going, smooth and silky, fat and comfortable Christianity so fashionable today. I hope we are willing to let the truth get hold of us, even at the cost of rejection or embarrassment.

The faith of the heavenly overcomers cost them everything and gained them everything. What of our faith?

9

The Supernatural Acts—
Blow Your Trumpets

When he opened the seventh seal, there was silence in heaven for about half an hour.

And I saw the seven angels who stand before God, and to them were given seven trumpets.

Another angel, who had a golden censer, came and stood at the altar. He was given much incense to offer, with the prayers of all the saints, on the golden altar before the throne. The smoke of the incense, together with the prayers of the saints, went up before God from the angel's hand. Then the angel took the censer, filled it with fire from the altar, and hurled it on the earth; and there came peals of thunder, rumblings, flashes of lightning and an earthquake....

The first angel sounded his trumpet, and there came hail and fire mixed with blood, and it was hurled down upon the earth. A third of the earth was burned up, a third of the trees were burned up, and all the green grass was burned up.

The second angel sounded his trumpet, and something like a huge mountain, all ablaze, was thrown into the sea. A third of the sea turned into

> *blood, a third of the living creatures in the sea died,*
> *and a third of the ships were destroyed.*
>
> *The third angel sounded his trumpet, and a great*
> *star, blazing like a torch, fell from the sky on a third*
> *of the rivers and on the springs of water... A third*
> *of the waters turned bitter, and many people died*
> *from the waters that had become bitter.*
>
> *The fourth angel sounded his trumpet, and a*
> *third of the sun was struck, a third of the moon, and*
> *a third of the stars, so that a third of them turned*
> *dark. A third of the day was without light, and also*
> *a third of the night.*
>
> Revelation 8:1–12

The human race has always been quick to blame the
world's disasters and tragedies—floods, famines,
plagues—on 'natural causes'. But in the end of the age
when the final judgements of God begin to fall, how long
will it be until people confess that there is another real,
though invisible, force in operation? Truly the wrath of
God will leave no hiding place for sinning men and
women.

We are told by John the apostle of the mighty
trumpets God gives to the seven angels 'who stand
before [him]', and of the dreadful woes descending upon
the earth as the trumpets begin to sound. I link these
events to the climactic period throughout the earth when
the antichrist has prevailed by means of deceit and force,
enslaving the major portion of the world and violating
every natural and spiritual law. Even then, as the judgements of God are being felt, I have no doubt that people
will offer 'rational explanations' for what is transpiring
and logical excuses for their not taking heed.

God has spoken to us in a variety of ways. Our general response has been, 'We did not hear His voice. We did not hear anything!' John recorded in his Gospel the reactions of an audience who heard God speak audibly. When Jesus talked of His coming death, asking God to glorify His name through it, 'a voice came from heaven, "I have glorified it, and will glorify it again"' (John 12:28). And what were the reactions of the bystanders? 'The crowd that was there and heard it said it had thundered; others said an angel had spoken to him' (12:29).

People prefer their logic, their powers of reason. Even when God speaks, they refuse to recognise His voice. They will not confess that God has spoken through Jesus Christ, the eternal Son. When He confronts them with their sin, they consult a psychiatrist and hope they can get their personalities 'properly adjusted'. But in a coming day, every knee will bow and every tongue will confess that Jesus Christ is Lord of all.

First, however, the trumpets of God will have sounded!

A supernatural transfer

This time, there will be no question in people's minds. When God shakes loose the world from Satan's control, shakes it loose from the rational scientists and the expedient politicians, shakes it loose from the pleasure lovers, He will turn it over to the one to whom it belongs—Jesus Christ! And He will do this in such a way that it will say to everyone on the earth: 'This is a supernatural manifestation! This is the God of the entire universe speaking!'

When God is finally ready to refine and restore the earth, everyone in heaven and on earth and in hell will know that no human laboratory could compound the fire that will be poured out on the earth. God has promised that He will not hide His wrath for ever. He is prepared to speak. And when He does, men will know that Oak Ridge scientists or Russian technologists could not produce these woes.

But before we come to God's judgements on our world, I need to make an important observation concerning the prayers of the people of God. Frequently I have heard Christians admit, 'I am discouraged. I have prayed and prayed—and nothing has happened!'

John sees an angel with a golden censer standing at the heavenly altar. He was given 'much incense', which he offered 'with the prayers of all the saints' on the golden altar before the heavenly throne (8:3). And 'the smoke of the incense, together with the prayers of the saints, went up before God from the angel's hand'.

It is right and proper that we who are the people of God should be giving ourselves to prayer. In Matthew 6:9-10, we read that Jesus taught His disciples to pray:

> Our Father in heaven,
> hallowed be your name,
> your kingdom come,
> your will be done
> on earth as it is in heaven.

Ever since, the believing saints of God have been praying the disciples' prayer: 'Your kingdom come.' That prayer cannot be answered—God's kingdom cannot come on earth—until God has shaken loose the usurpers who hold this world in their power and control. But in God's time the world will be restored to Jesus Christ who created it and bought it back with His own precious blood.

A delayed response

I sense in this picture in Revelation that some of our prayers on that altar have been acknowledged, but God has purposely delayed His response. Those yet unanswered prayers of ours are being kept there at the altar that they may be mingled with the divine incense and thus become effective before God's throne. And now at last the moment has come. It is time for the fire from the altar to be hurled upon the earth as God's judgements continue.

There is still much about prayer and intercession that we do not understand. Probably we will continue to feel that our prayers often seem to be ineffective. It is my counsel, based on this episode, that our prayers *are* useful to God and effective. But God, for His own purposes, may hold them for a time before He answers.

Think of the kernels of grain, the seed, that the farmer plants in the ground in the autumn. How patient the farmer must be! Throughout the long, cold winter the seed is dormant. There is no evidence at all that it is there—covered by the cold earth itself. The snows come and go. The ground freezes and thaws. Does the farmer lie awake at night worrying that those seeds he placed in the ground might be ineffective? He does not. He knows that spring will come!

And in due course, the sunshine of March or April warms the air. Spring rains water the ground. The farmer knows then that it will not be long until green shoots suddenly break out from their covering of earth. And in their own time, great waving fields of grain are ready for the harvest. The farmer's faith in the seed he planted is fully justified.

Likewise, God wants us to be patient with every prayer and petition we sincerely send up to that heavenly

altar. Our praying done in the Spirit cannot be ineffective. It is as though God is saying to us: 'You have
planted the seed. You have prayed for My will to be
done and for My kingdom to come on earth. Your
prayers will be mingled with the divine incense. The fire
from the altar will fall upon the earth, and God's desire
will be communicated to men and women. The effective
prayers of my Son, Jesus, will join with the effective
prayers of righteous men and women. Be patient and put
your trust in Me, day by day!'

The unexplained silence

You will note, as we return to the opening verse of
chapter 8, that after the seventh seal was opened 'there
was silence in heaven for about half an hour'. It will do
you no good to ask me, 'What does this silence in heaven
mean?' I would tell you if I knew—but I do not know. It
does indicate a pause, perhaps a kind of divine 'Selah' in
heaven, as though the wheels of judgement have ground
to a merciful stop for a brief time.

John himself does not try to explain or interpret the
heavenly silence. Instead, he proceeds to the next event
in his vision:

> And I saw the seven angels who stand before God, and to
> them were given seven trumpets. . . . And there came peals
> of thunder, rumblings, flashes of lightning and an earth-
> quake.
>
> *8:2,5*

John describes this heavenly phenomena taking place
even before the seven angels sounded their trumpets of
woe. Earlier, in his vision of the heavenly throne, John
reported the 'flashes of lightning, rumblings and peals of

thunder' that came from the throne (4:5). I believe John is telling us in chapter 8 that the heavenly manifestations of justice and judgement first seen and heard at the throne of God have now reached the earth. The crucial time of trial and tribulation for mankind has come.

It is well for us to review here what we know about the trumpets of God in the Bible. The blowing of trumpets is mentioned in the Scriptures 125 times. God instructed His people Israel to use trumpets for warnings, to call an assembly and to announce the feast days. Trumpets were also to be used to mobilise for war. The Old Testament prophets, speaking by the Spirit of God, used the figure of the sounding trumpet in their appeals to a backslidden nation: 'Blow the trumpet in Zion: sound the alarm, warn the people!'

Paul, addressing the Corinthian believers concerning the end of the age and the return of Christ for His living saints and the resurrected Christian dead, had this to say:

> Listen, I tell you a mystery: We will not all sleep, but we will all be changed—in a flash, in the twinkling of an eye, at the last trumpet. For the trumpet will sound, the dead will be raised imperishable, and we will be changed.
>
> *1 Corinthians 15:51–52*

Why the talk of judgement?

Men and women, absorbed in their human contentment, will ask, 'Why should there be the sounding trumpets? Why should there be such warnings? Why the talk of impending judgement?'

I will tell you why. God once walked and conversed with the man and woman He had created. He spoke to

them in the Garden of Eden in the cool of the day in the
quiet voice of love.

And the man and the woman, walking among the
trees of the garden, heard His voice and responded.

But Adam and Eve sinned, and since then their
descendants have chosen not to listen for God's voice.
Men and women could hear the voice of God if they
would. By choice they do not.

As we noted earlier, lost humanity's cup of iniquity is
brim full. The figure is alarming, frightening. God
watches as the cup fills. Then, suddenly, it is an over-
flowing cup, and God summons His seven trumpeters to
action:

> The first angel sounded his trumpet, and there came hail
> and fire mixed with blood, and it was hurled down upon the
> earth. A third of the earth was burned up, a third of the
> trees were burned up, and all the green grass was burned
> up.
>
> 8:7

People have always loved fire, and God will say,
'Blow the trumpet—and give them all the fire they want!'

> The second angel sounded his trumpet, and something like a
> huge mountain, all ablaze, was thrown into the sea. A third
> of the sea turned into blood, a third of the living creatures in
> the sea died, and a third of the ships were destroyed.
>
> 8:8–9

People have always been prone to shed the blood of
their fellows, and God will say, 'Blow the trumpet—and
give them all the blood they can take!'

> The third angel sounded his trumpet, and a great star,

blazing like a torch, fell from the sky on a third of the rivers
and on the springs of water—the name of the star is Worm-
wood. A third of the waters turned bitter, and many people
died from the waters that had become bitter.

8:10–11

People have always dealt with each other in bitterness. God will say, 'Blow the trumpet—and give them
bitterness, even more bitterness than they want!'

The fourth angel sounded his trumpet, and a third of the sun
was struck, a third of the moon, and a third of the stars, so
that a third of them turned dark. A third of the day was
without light, and also a third of the night.

8:12

People have always loved their deeds of darkness.
God will say, 'Blow the trumpet—and give them darkness and confusion and woe!'

Judgements beyond mankind's doing

For sure, these will be manifestations of the wrath and
the power of God that cannot be mistaken for anything
humans are capable of doing. I wonder about some of
the human presumptions in our day. I wonder—but I do
not have the answers. I wonder if some of God's judgements will take place because of our arrogant presumptions inherent in our invasions into God's creation
secrets, including the realm of space.

I do not have any scriptural grounds for saying this,
but I do wonder if God will finally take His sponge,
apply His own divine detergent and mop not only earth
but sky, cleansing space of its human contamination.

As if the previous four judgements were insufficient,

God issues a warning concerning what follows. John says,

> As I watched, I heard an eagle that was flying in mid-air call out in a loud voice: 'Woe! Woe! Woe to the inhabitants of the earth, because of the trumpet blasts about to be sounded by the other three angels!'
>
> 8:13

All of what I have reviewed in this chapter pertains to an awesome day yet future. By the goodness and the grace of God, you and I today are not hearing those trumpet blasts of final woe and judgement.

Today we hear an entirely different voice. It is the voice of Jesus calling wandering sinners home, assuring them that God is still honouring repentance and faith and obedience! It is the voice of Jesus, as gentle as the voice of a mother calling to her first-born. He says, 'Come to me, all you who are weary and burdened' (Matthew 11:28).

God intends for us to hear

Fellow Christian, it is God's will and God's plan that we hear His voice. It is the voice of Jesus, the voice of the Holy Spirit and the counsel of the Scriptures that we should not be overcome with the complexities and cares of our daily lives.

> Heaven and earth will pass away, but my words will never pass away.
>
> Be careful, or your hearts will be weighed down with dissipation, drunkenness and the anxieties of life, and that day will close on you unexpectedly like a trap. For it will

come upon all those who live on the face of the whole earth.
Luke 21:33–35

Doctors warn us that we in the West eat too much, drink too much, sleep too much, worry too much. More of us suffer from mental illness than suffer from major physical illness. We are selfish and self-centred. We want too many pleasures and too few responsibilities. We who are believers are prone to think we will hear the trumpets of woe in time to do something about all of this. But at that time, it will be too late!

The voice of God today is a quiet voice. The voice of God's love and grace is constant—never strident, never compulsive. God has sent His messengers to every generation. He has spoken through the urgent voice of the prophet. He has spoken through the concerned voice of the preacher and the evangelist. He has spoken through the sweet voice of the gospel singer. He has spoken through the voices of plain, sincere, loving men and women who have given faithful witness to the transforming new birth from above and the joys that God's children will know throughout the eternity to come.

These voices from God have consistently proclaimed:

> Wake up, O sleeper,
> rise from the dead,
> and Christ will shine on you.
> *Ephesians 5:14*

These voices repeat the offer of our Lord:

Take my yoke upon you and learn from me, for I am gentle and humble in heart, and you will find rest for your souls.
Matthew 11:29

I am a troubled pastor

I confess that, as a pastor, I am a troubled man. I am concerned. It is too late in my ministry for me to be engaged week after week with men and women who do not hear the pleading voice of God for our time and for our condition. I am serious about this. I do wonder if God must turn from those who have heard all of the Bible truths over and over again in order to find willing and responsive listeners elsewhere.

In our basic evangelicalism we disagree with that. We assure ourselves that God is always waiting to bless us. I remind you that the Jews of Jesus' day held to the same attitude. 'Do not worry about us,' they said in effect. 'We are Abraham's descendants. We know who we are. If God is going to bless anyone, He is going to bless us!' Remember what Jesus said to them: 'If you were Abraham's children,...then you would do the things Abraham did' (John 8:39). If they were Abraham's descendants, He was saying, they would act like Abraham and not be trying to kill their promised Messiah.

I cannot determine when I will die. But I hope I do not live to see the day when God has to turn from men and women who have heard His holy truth and have played with it, fooled with it and equated it with fun and entertainment and religious nonsense.

We cannot deny that this attitude is found in much of current Christianity. As a result, people have hardened their hearts to the point that they no longer hear the voice of God.

We ought to be crying out in repentance and prayer: 'Oh God, we have heard so much of Your truth, over and over again, yet we are ashamed that we have done so little in giving You our devotion and obedience!'

May God have mercy on us!

10

The Human Resolution—
We Will Not Repent

The fifth angel sounded his trumpet, and I saw a star that had fallen from the sky to the earth. The star was given the key to the shaft of the Abyss. When he opened the Abyss, smoke rose from it like the smoke from a gigantic furnace. The sun and sky were darkened by the smoke from the Abyss. And out of the smoke locusts came down upon the earth and were given power like that of scorpions of the earth. They were told not to harm the grass of the earth or any plant or tree, but only those people who did not have the seal of God on their foreheads. They were not given power to kill them, but only to torture them for five months. And the agony they suffered was like that of the sting of a scorpion when it strikes a man. During those days men will seek death, but will not find it; they will long to die, but death will elude them. . . .

The sixth angel blew his trumpet, and I heard a voice coming from the horns of the golden altar that is before God. It said to the sixth angel who had the trumpet, 'Release the four angels who are bound at the great river Euphrates.' And the four angels who

*had been kept ready for this very hour and day and
month and year were released to kill a third of
mankind. The number of the mounted troops was
two hundred million. I heard their number....*

*The rest of mankind that were not killed by these
plagues still did not repent of the work of their
hands; they did not stop worshipping demons, and
idols of gold, silver, bronze, stone and wood—idols
that cannot see or hear or walk.*

Revelation 9:1–6, 13–15, 20

Everything I read these days tells me we are experienc-
ing a great new wave of interest in spiritism and devil
worship. I take this as one of the signs that God's age of
grace and mercy is approaching the end point. It is
evidence that the time may be near when He proclaims:
'I have seen enough of mankind's sin, rebellion and
perversion. It is time for the trumpets of judgement to
sound!'

John's record in the ninth chapter of the Revelation is
a sombre, disturbing portrayal of judgement. It is a
prophecy of destruction and desolation that cannot be
anything but revolting to humans who deny that God has
any right to judge and punish their rebellion against His
love and His will. To us who believe that God is good
and that He originally made us in His image, we discern
a further message. He is saying that there is another
world, another kingdom, that is always keeping an eye
on this world we inhabit!

If we are willing to add this message from the Revelation to the weight of other Scriptures, we discover God
saying to us that the earth on which we live is not self-
explanatory and certainly not self-sufficient. This earth
on which we spin is only a shadow of the real, though

invisible, world above. Although our earth is largely peopled by a rebel race, it had a divine origin. And God is about to enforce His claim upon it and judge those who are usurpers.

Humans, deceived by the devil and charmed by their own pride and abilities, deny that our world is a rebel province in God's universe. They deny that human society has willfully pulled loose from God's rule and the rest of God's domain. In fact, they deny that men and women are the creation of God. They deny even that they owe any allegiance to God, their Creator.

Worst of all, in my opinion, these rebels deny that they will be obliged to settle their debt with the Creator God at a time of His choosing!

The final settlement

John has been able to give us some indication of conditions and events that will take place on the earth as the hour of final settlement begins. He makes it clear that the visitation of judgement upon the earth will involve an invasion of supernatural powers. There will be fearsome creatures loosed upon the earth, and great segments of the population will not only suffer but will be slain in the process. Think together with me about the supernatural events.

I will have to confess that I am among those who have been consistently sceptical of the stories of 'flying saucers'. Likewise, I have never believed the tales people have told of sighting monstrous sea serpents. Although I have heard the legends concerning the diminutive leprechauns, I have never accepted the notion of their existence.

But I do believe that the supernatural is a part of

God's being and eternal existence. I am convinced that when the living Lord of Creation, the Almighty God, begins to bring this rebel world back into the divine orbit, there will be an invasion from the world above as well as from the world below. And once the trumpets have sounded, sinful men and women will have no recourse. Neither will they have questions as to the origin of the judgement. There will be no need for a governmental inquiry or investigation. All will know that they have come to the time of God's judgement throughout the world.

As God sends these strange, punishing creatures upon the earth, there will be two human reactions. Some people will attempt suicide—only to discover that suicide is impossible: 'They will long to die, but death will elude them' (9:6). Some will continue stubbornly in their sinful practices: '[They] still did not repent;...they did not stop worshipping demons, and idols....Nor did they repent of their murders, their magic arts, their sexual immorality or their thefts' (9:20–21).

The God of heaven and earth, as He makes His just claims, will be saying to a rebellious, lost race: 'You speak of the great "natural" forces you have experienced. You know about the release of nuclear power and boast of your intelligence in discovering the secrets of fusion and fission. But as your Creator, I am forewarning you that you have not seen anything at all. Although you have become used to living in the midst of sin and violence in a tear-stained and terror-filled world, you have not seen anything to compare with the blood and fire and devastation and death that will signal the end of My grace and mercy!'

Specific details omitted

John does not give us some of the specific details. For
example, we cannot here pin-point the time of the rapture of the believing church. John does give us one clue,
however—the locust-like creatures with scorpion
stingers were instructed not to hurt men and women who
had the seal of God in their foreheads. The living saints
will be marked and protected for the little time they will
yet be on earth. But the wicked and the unbelieving will
be tormented by these invading creatures until they will
want to die. And even that desperate respite will be
denied them—they will not even be able to 'end it all'.

In John's vision, there was a sixth trumpet blast. John
heard a voice coming from the horns of the golden altar
before God, saying, 'Release the four angels' (9:14).
And the four angels who had been in readiness for this
moment were released 'to kill a third of mankind'. They
accomplished their gruesome assignment by means of
'mounted troops' numbering 'two hundred million'.
John adds: 'The heads of the horses resembled the heads
of lions, and out of their mouths came fire, smoke and
sulphur. A third of mankind was killed by the three
plagues of fire, smoke and sulphur that came out of their
mouths.'

Now, I am aware that there are many people—even
some Christians—who do not believe these judgements
and torments will actually happen. They may discount
the Revelation, arguing that the imagery is hard to interpret, but what will they do with the words and warnings
of our Lord Jesus Christ? Here is what *He* said:

Watch out that no-one deceives you.... You will hear of
wars and rumours of wars, but see to it that you are not
alarmed.... Nation will rise against nation, and kingdom

against kingdom. There will be famines and earthquakes in various places. All these are the beginning of birth pains.

Then you will be handed over to be persecuted and put to death, and you will be hated by all nations because of me. At that time many will turn away from the faith and will betray and hate each other....

There will be great distress, unequalled from the beginning of the world until now—and never to be equalled again. If those days had not been cut short, no-one would survive, but for the sake of the elect those days will be shortened....

Immediately after the distress of those days 'the sun will be darkened, and the moon will not give its light; the stars will fall from the sky, and the heavenly bodies will be shaken.'

Matthew 24:4–29

Confirmed by prophets and apostles

Students of the Bible are aware that the Old Testament prophets and the writing apostles of New Testament times foresaw and proclaimed God's coming day of judgement—the consummate settling of accounts between the sovereign God and His rebellious and sinful creation.

Throughout the centuries, saints whom God has touched with heavenly fire from His altar have woven this concept of accountability and judgement into a discernible tapestry. In our day, we have seen the vision dimly, and we can only confess that we do not understand it all. I have said it before. Let us not get involved in trying to decipher all the minute details of God's plans. The great central truth is what matters: When God gets enough of this world's sin and violence and rebellion, He will do something about it!

God intends to restore the unity of His creation. He

will sort out good from bad. He will halt the infection of evil. He will balance the scales of justice.

Jesus Christ revealed to John the broad outline of God's wrathful judgement. We sense a progression in the breaking of the seals, in the sounding of the trumpets, in the pouring out of the vials, in the appearance of the four horsemen. We do not need to know the details. God has said He will use every means to shake loose the rebellious forces that have laid claim to His earth.

How desperately we would like to believe that in the face of such world-wide judgements, all lost men and women will cry out to God, 'We have been wrong! We repent! We confess our evil deeds! We want to join those whose faith and trust is in God!'

I repeat: We would like to believe that judgement will bring unbelievers to God. But such will not be the case. 'The rest of mankind that were not killed by these plagues still did not repent' (9:20).

Repentance is our moral obligation

All my adult life I have been a student of the Bible. Among other things, it is the record of how God deals with mankind. I can draw but one conclusion from my research: *All people are morally obligated to repent and to ask forgiveness of God.* Failing to do that, they will perish. In the course of my ministry I have talked to people who thought they would be doing God a big favour if they would repent. The fact is, men and women who repent and return to God are simply doing what they *should* do as beings once created in God's likeness.

It should not be a surprise to us when John reports that people who have just seen a third of the world's population perish in divine judgement will continue to rebel against God. We live amid a proud, selfish and self-sufficient people. Even in our Christian churches there are those who want to be known as 'respectable church members'—and not as lost sinners who have had to confess their guilt before God. How infrequently do we hear of genuine repentance! When repentance is real and faith is genuine, the atoning death of Jesus Christ is effective for pardon.

But the sad lesson from the Scriptures is plain. Sinful, rebellious people can never be forced to repent. The same act that may cause one person to repent and believe will cause others to hate and despise God. The same Bible sermon that brings one person to tearful submission at an altar of prayer will send others out with pride and a resolve to have their own human way.

If we are close enough to God in our spiritual life and desires, we want Him to do something about present-day lawless rebellion. We recognise it as blasphemy against the high King of Heaven. But even some Christians do not want God to do anything that will bring judgement or suffering. Can we be unconcerned about bringing this world to a final accounting before God? If our hearts beat with the heart of God, should we not cry out within ourselves, 'Oh God, do send Your judgements! Let Your judgements be revealed in Your time and in Your own measure!'

There are things worse than death

Death is not the worst thing that can happen to a person! I recall the first time I heard that statement. I was in a quiet conversation with Harry M. Shuman, for many years president of The Christian and Missionary

Alliance. He was a soft-spoken, yet forceful man of God, rich in the wisdom of God's word. We were talking of the serious issues of life and death. When he had something especially important to say, Dr Shuman had an unusual way of lowering his voice and tilting his head just a bit. I can see him yet as he looked out from under his shaggy brows straight into my eyes. 'Remember, Tozer, death is not the worst thing that can happen to a person!'

For the Christian, death is a journey to the eternal world. It is a victory, a rest, a delight. I am sure my small amount of physical suffering in life has been mild compared with Paul's. But I think I have some understanding of what he meant when he told the Philippians: 'To me, to live is Christ and to die is gain.... I desire to depart and be with Christ, which is better by far....' (Philippians 1:21,23). The more a Christian suffers in the body, the more he or she thinks about the triumph of going home to heaven.

But we modern Christians seem to be a strange breed. We are so completely satisfied with the earthly things we have collected, and we so enjoy this age's creature comforts, that we would rather stay here for a long, long time! Probably we do not tell God about that kind of desire when we pray. We know it would not be considered pious or spiritual if people knew we preferred our position here to the prospect of heaven.

For years I have made a practice of writing many of my earnest prayers to God in a little book—a book now well worn. I still turn often to the petitions I recorded in that book. I remind God often of what my prayers have been.

One prayer in the book—and God knows it well by this time, for I pray it often—goes like this:

Oh God, let me die rather than to go on day by day living wrong. I do not want to become a careless, fleshly old man. I want to be right so that I can die right. Lord, I do not want my life to be extended if it would mean that I should cease to live right and fail in my mission to glorify You all of my days!

An Old Testament example

Long ago, Hezekiah, king of Judah, became ill and God told him he would die. The king turned his face to the wall and sulked. Then he asked the Lord, in effect, 'Why me? I have cleansed the temple, and we have had a revival. Because of me, the nation has become closer to You'.

As you will recall from 2 Kings 20, the Lord gave Hezekiah a fifteen-year extension of life. Restored to health and vigour, Hezekiah disgraced himself and dishonoured God before he died and was buried.

I would not want an extra fifteen years in which to backslide and dishonour my Lord. I would rather go home right now than to live on—if living on was to be a waste of God's time and my own!

We look at the deteriorating condition of our world. We consider the godless life-styles of so many millions of the world's people. Then we reflect on the devastating future judgements prophesied in the Revelation and elsewhere in God's word. Harry M. Shuman was right: For the sincere followers of the Lamb, death is not the worst thing that can happen to them.

11

The Command— No More Delay

Then I saw another mighty angel coming down from heaven. He was robed in a cloud, with a rainbow above his head; his face was like the sun, and his legs were like fiery pillars. He was holding a little scroll, which lay open in his hand. He planted his right foot on the sea and his left foot on the land, and he gave a loud shout like the roar of a lion. When he shouted, the voices of the seven thunders spoke. And when the seven thunders spoke, I was about to write; but I heard a voice from heaven say, 'Seal up what the seven thunders have said and do not write it down.'

Then the angel I had seen standing on the sea and on the land raised his right hand to heaven And he swore by him who lives for ever and ever, who created the heavens and all that is in them, the earth and all that is in it, and the sea and all that is in it, and said, 'There will be no more delay! But in the days when the seventh angel is about to sound his trumpet, the mystery of God will be accomplished, just as he announced to his servants the prophets.'

Revelation 10:1–7

131

If you have ever watched a basketball or a football game, you know that when a team calls 'Time out!' there will be a pause, a time of waiting. If the coach or manager wants to communicate a message to the players, he calls 'Time out!' At that point, everything comes to a temporary halt. That is the rule of the contest.

The game clock stops. The ball is inactive. There can be no scoring. 'Time out!' is a period of waiting until the referee blows the whistle, calling the players back to their positions so that the game can continue. When that whistle blows, the referee actually is announcing, 'There will be no more delay!'

I use that illustration to make plain the meaning of the activity related in Revelation 10. One of God's mighty angels proclaims to the entire creation: 'There will be no more delay! The God who lives for ever and ever, the God who created the heavens and the earth and the sea, will now bring to pass all that He has planned on behalf of His creation. There will be no more delay!'

For years we have read this announcement in the King James Version of the Bible, where the wording is 'There should be time no longer'. In our hymns and gospel songs we have made wide use of that phrase, singing about time being no more, looking forward to a period when time will cease. But actually, that great angel messenger was proclaiming, 'The time-out is ending. The long pause is over. There will be no more delay. The living God is now prepared to reveal the consummation of all things!'

Now, if any of us who believe the Bible and are expecting the Lord's return should be granted an audience before the United Nations assembly and should start to explain God's plan for the consummation of this age, we would be booed and hooted out of that impressive hall! We would quickly be evicted—and not just by atheistic Russians or Chinese, but by American, Canadian and British delegates, too! We will never get a hearing at the United Nations for God's plans. But the prophetic word of David and Isaiah and Daniel and Paul and Peter still stands. These men were not mistaken in their faith. And, thankfully, the words of our Lord Jesus Christ will stand!

Daniel predicted the consummation

Consider God's last words to Daniel at the end of his prophetic record. By then, Daniel was old and weary, but all his life he had been God's faithful servant. God said:

> Go your way, Daniel, because the words are closed up and sealed until the time of the end. Many will be purified, made spotless and refined, but the wicked will continue to be wicked. None of the wicked will understand, but those who are wise will understand. . . .
>
> As for you, go your way till the end. You will rest, and then at the end of the days you will rise to receive your allotted inheritance.
>
> *Daniel 12:9–13*

As far as we know, Daniel died a natural death. But many of the prophets died violent deaths because of their faith. Consider, too, the Christian martyrs of the past centuries. You should be familiar with their lives, if you are not. Their testimonies will always stand. They forfeited physical life in the calm and joyful belief that God is faithful and that He will make all things right in the consummation that is yet ahead. They knew that sin and greed and hatred were in control for a time, but their destination was their Father's house, and they knew that everything up there has always been all right!

These martyrs were aware that God had called a 'Time out!' for His own good reasons. It was not that God had abandoned His plan, worked out from the foundation of the world. His plan is perfect—God's nature assures us of that, even as we wait. This present delay is a time of mercy, a window of salvation.

God's great plan for the salvation of our lost race deals with mankind's sinfulness and with God's own holiness and justice. There can be little argument about what sin has done to the human race. The Bible speaks of our life as a cup with a certain capacity. As long as we sin against God, the cup continues to fill. We sin and we sin and we sin! We seem to be of the opinion that God does not really take notice of our rebellion against Him.

But the sins are cumulative. That is the terrible thing about transgression. Sin in the human nature builds. It grows and grows. Finally our propensity for evil reaches the point of overflow, and then the judgement of God must fall.

There was a time in history when the wickedness of the nations had built to the point of overflow. God's righteous judgement should have fallen on all of mankind. But at that crucial point of time, Jesus Christ, the eternal Son, the Lamb of God Himself, came to earth and gave His life, opening wide the gates of heaven. Through the atoning death of our Saviour, God was able to extend pardon to all who came to Jesus in faith, appealing for mercy.

The God of all mercy in effect called a divine 'Time out!' While His eternal Son is actively interceding at His right hand, God's cataclysmic judgement upon our world will be delayed.

Bible scholars call the tenth chapter of the Revelation 'parenthetical'. By that they mean that, although significant, it does not advance the progress of events in the entire book. But as I ponder this heavenly scene, my heart is lifted up! I do not know what it does for you, but it gets me out of the dull earth, where cares abound, and transports me into another world. I do not have to understand it all to be blessed and helped. The Revelation is rich, rewarding, awesome! It is at once magnificent and terrible, noble and frightening.

We must not lose sight of the fact that this record primarily is the Revelation of Jesus Christ. When you look up into the heavens at night, you may see an especially bright star, but you cannot help seeing as well many of the other stars surrounding it. In the Revelation we have primarily the Revelation of Jesus Christ Himself. He is first. He is 'of the Father's love begotten'. Jesus is the one by whom the race is to be redeemed, the earth restored, evil vanquished, Satan defeated, justice established, the alienation between God and us ended. Jesus split apart the curtain that separated us from God.

Yet, when we look fully at Jesus, we see also much that surrounds Him. We take note, for instance, of the angels of heaven, the reality of hell and the great abyss, the throne of God, the souls of the righteous, the last judgement, the marriage supper of the Lamb, the new heavens and the new earth.

Do not be frightened by the symbols

I have mentioned before the use of symbols in the Revelation. Figures of speech abound throughout the Bible. We should not let the use of symbolism frighten us away. That is one of the devil's neatest tricks—getting

believers to suppose there is so much in the word of God
that they cannot understand that they neglect *all* of the
word of God. My advice: Go to the Bible itself. You will
find that it interprets itself.

For example, John saw the angel 'robed in a cloud'.
Do you suppose that could be a cloud as we know
clouds? Clouds are composed of water. They make poor
robes. But go back into the life and history of Israel,
God's chosen people. In the wilderness Israel followed
the divine cloud by day and the pillar of fire by night.
The cloud and the fire were the 'Shekinah'—the presence of Almighty God with His pilgrim people. That was
the glory of God. Again, when the risen Christ was taken
away into Heaven, a cloud received Him out of their
sight. In the Scriptures a cloud means the visible manifestation of the invisible God.

When this mighty angel came forth from the throne of
God, John saw his robe as that of a cloud. Something of
the splendour and glory of God at His throne clung to
the angel as he moved from the heavenly scene to command the judgements of God on the earth. There was a
rainbow above his head. His face was like the sun. His
legs were like fiery pillars. As a mighty messenger from
God, he planted his right foot on the sea and his left foot
on the land. When he shouted, it was like the roar of a
lion, and in the midst of it all, John heard as well the
voices of 'the seven thunders' (10:3).

John tells us he was about to write down what the
seven thunders said, but a voice from heaven ordered,
'Seal up what the seven thunders have said' (10:4). Some
people are curious as to the message of the seven
thunders. They have a hard time letting the matter rest.
They want to know.

I have a feeling that sometime in our eternal future we

are going to know the message spoken by the thunders. For now, we must leave it at that. It was a message sealed up for a later time. Of one thing I am confident; it was a message spoken in favour of God and His Christ; it was a message on the side of righteousness, faithfulness and holiness.

Do you not think God expects us to focus on the more important issues? Why should we spend time over obscure, curious elements? God has given us sixty-six books within our Bible to prepare us for the coming events that will signal the return of Christ and the judgement of the nations. Heeding what we *know* to do will keep us well occupied.

Decisive action

The mighty angel whom John saw raised his right hand to the heavens. He knew the time had come. He knew authority had been given to him. He raised his right hand in acknowledgement of the God above, whom he worshipped and served.

I like that! We have too many weak personalities on earth who always leave something undone. They are afraid to take final, decisive action. As a result, they do not accomplish the goals they have set. With the poet we say, 'We are such little men when the stars come out!'

Yes, I like this picture John has given us. The mighty angel knows his task and his authority. He raises his right hand to heaven and in the name of the eternal God cries out, 'The time has come! There will be no more delay!'

When the time comes for that announcement, three worlds will hear it. Heaven will hear it, with full agreement that the time of judgement has indeed come. The underworld of hell will hear the shout, and there will be fright. And on earth, the saints of God, the believing body of Christ, will hear it and be glad!

We are living in a period when God waits in grace and mercy. In His faithfulness, God is calling out a people for His name—those who will repent and believe, those who will cast their lot with Jesus Christ. When the mighty angel shouts his signal and raises his hand heavenward, it will be eternally too late. Only God can say when iniquity overflows, when the time is ripe.

The event is certain; the timing is uncertain. Those facts constitute one of the compelling reasons for my strong belief in the cause of world missions. I am thankful to be a part of a missionary-minded church. I believe involvement in God's programme of calling out a people world-wide for His name is of primary importance. The church is not simply a religious institution. It is not a religious theatre where performers are paid to amuse those who attend. It is an assembly of redeemed sinners—men and women called unto Christ and commissioned to spread His gospel to the ends of the earth.

Then, at a time known only to God, the end of the age will come and Jesus Christ will return to earth for His own believing and faithful people—His church.

Yes, Jesus Christ *will* return

I am not surprised that I still meet people who do not believe in the return of Christ. Some of them, in fact, armed with Bibles, would like to set me straight. Not too long after an editorial appeared in which I quoted the apostle Paul, I heard from a professor who told me I had it all wrong. Paul did not mean what I had said he meant as I applied his statement to present-day life.

I took time to write a reply. 'When it comes to saying

what he meant,' I began, 'Paul's batting average has been pretty good up to now. So I will string along with what Paul plainly, clearly said.' I did not figure I needed someone to straighten me out—especially someone who had decided the Bible does not mean what it says.

When the Bible says God is calling a special people out of the nations to bear His name, I believe it! When the Bible declares His name is Jesus and His people are Christians—Christ's ones—I believe that, too! No one is going to argue me out of my faith in what God has said. As far as I am concerned, it is a fact that Jesus is coming again. The question I raise is this: Are we prepared spiritually for His coming? Are we tolerating conditions in our midst that will cause us embarrassment when He comes?

In the evangelical church, we have come through a period when nearly everyone believed and taught the same thing concerning our preparation for Christ's return. There has been just one prerequisite to readiness: being born again. Being born again is almost like receiving a pass to a special event. When Jesus returns, we whip out the pass to prove our readiness!

Frankly, I do not think it will be at all like that. I do not believe that all of the professed believers are automatically ready to meet the Lord. If being born again was the only prerequisite, I must ask why Peter and Paul and John and our Lord exhorted, warned, pleaded that we should live and watch and pray so as to be *ready* for Jesus' coming? If we are automatically ready, why does our Lord admonish the Philadelphia church to hold tenaciously to their faith and strength 'so that no-one will take [their] crown' (3:11)?

God demands spiritual preparation

Our pious forefathers believed in spiritual preparation,
and they said so. They saw themselves as a bride being
prepared to meet the bridegroom. They regarded this
earth as the dressing room to outfit them for heaven.
They were well aware of God's admonition to personal
holiness even as He was holy.

Why are we so slow to admit that our Lord Jesus
Christ taught that He would accomplish His great task of
church building through spiritually gifted men and
women? His New Testament promises are so plain that
no one can misunderstand them. It was His word that we
should 'receive power' through the infusion of His Spirit
in our lives.

I have mentioned the necessity for spiritual preparation in light of the coming of our Lord Jesus Christ. Such
preparation is related as well to spiritual responsibility.
Too many professing Christians will not accept responsibility. They are woefully mistaken in their theology
when they excuse themselves by insisting that 'Jesus did
all the dying and we get all the benefits—without any
responsibility'. I think they must have fallen short in
their Bible study.

One aspect of Christ's coming is our solemn
appearance before His judgement seat, at which time we
shall 'receive what is due [us] for the things done while in
the body, whether good or bad' (2 Corinthians 5:10).
What we have done for our own glory will be exposed to
our embarrassment. Our supposed accomplishments
achieved without the direction of the Holy Spirit will be
blown away as worthless stubble. In that final day of
review and examination, only that which has been
wrought by the Spirit of God will endure as eternal
treasure.

The pursuit of godliness

It pains me every time I hear Christians excusing their shallow, carnal living with a 'We're doing the best we can!' The apostle Peter told the suffering Christians of his day that there was a far better testimony than that:

> Since everything will be destroyed in this way, what kind of people ought you to be? You ought to live holy and godly lives as you look forward to the day of God and speed its coming....
>
> Make every effort to be found spotless, blameless and at peace with him....
>
> Be on your guard so that you may not be carried away by the error of lawless men and fall from your secure position. But grow in the grace and knowledge of our Lord and Saviour Jesus Christ.
>
> *2 Peter 3:11–18*

Perhaps in light of that exhortation you feel as I do: that we need to drop off even some of the 'normal' things we are doing—things that may not of themselves be wrong, but things that are keeping us from the serious pursuit of godliness.

At that coming day, we shall not be sorry we did!

12

The Invitation—
Eat and Digest God's Word

*Then the voice that I had heard from heaven spoke
to me once more: 'Go, take the scroll that lies open
in the hand of the angel who is standing on the sea
and on the land.'*

*So I went to the angel and asked him to give me
the little scroll. He said to me, 'Take it and eat it. It
will turn your stomach sour, but in your mouth it
will be as sweet as honey.' I took the little scroll from
the angel's hand and ate it. It tasted as sweet as
honey in my mouth, but when I had eaten it, my
stomach turned sour. Then I was told, 'You must
prophesy again about many peoples, nations, lan-
guages and kings.'*

10:8–11

We are living in a time of soft, easy Christianity. It is an
era marked by a polite, weekly 'nibbling' around the
edges of the word of God. Our pews are filled with nice,
affable Christians who are willing to listen to outlines
from the Bible purporting to be sermons. But they fail to
absorb and digest the word so that it becomes their
controlling interest.

Any study of the Revelation will fall short of God's purpose if it does not make us more keenly aware of the eternal, unchanging nature of God's word to mankind. In God's realm, the saddest words of tongue or pen may well be, 'I failed to take God at His word.'

The tenth chapter concludes with the apostle John's testimony concerning a divine scroll. The divine scroll had to do with impending judgement upon our earth. The open scroll was in the hand of the strong angel who stood on land and sea. Instructed by a heavenly voice to ask for the open scroll, John did so. The angel was not only quite willing for John to have it, but he told John to *eat* the document, adding, 'It will turn your stomach sour, but in your mouth it will be as sweet as honey.' John followed the unusual instructions and found the angel's prediction accurate.

Now, a little scroll in John's day would be a little book in ours. So I am going to refer to the scroll as a book—a book of divine origin.

We have no way of knowing the full significance of the little book that John took from the hand of the angel. But there is considerable agreement among Bible students that it symbolises the word of God—or perhaps some particular part of the word of God. Such an interpretation agrees with other prophetic Scripture.

Jeremiah, Ezekiel

Jeremiah, for example, was given the difficult task of bearing word of God's impending judgement to Judah and Jerusalem. It would be an unwelcome message to those for whom it was destined:

'Who will have pity on you, O Jerusalem? Who will mourn

for you? Who will stop to ask how you are? You have rejected me,' declares the Lord. 'You keep on backsliding. So I will lay hands on you and destroy you; I can no longer show compassion.'

Jeremiah 15:5–6

Jeremiah was a willing messenger, but he was under no illusion concerning the response God's message would meet—or of his own vulnerability as the bearer of such tidings:

You understand, O Lord; remember me and care for me. Avenge me on my persecutors. You are long-suffering—do not take me away; think of how I suffer reproach for your sake.

15:15

Then Jeremiah added this interesting statement:

When your words came, I ate them; they were my joy and my heart's delight, for I bear your name, O Lord God Almighty.

15:16

Ezekiel had a similar experience when God commissioned him to prophesy to rebellious Israel:

[The voice] said to me, 'Son of man, stand up on your feet and I will speak to you.' As he spoke, the Spirit came into me and raised me to my feet, and I heard him speaking to me.

He said: 'Son of man, I am sending you to the Israelites, to a rebellious nation that has rebelled against me; they and their fathers have been in revolt against me to this very day....'

Then I looked, and I saw a hand stretched out to me. In it was a scroll, which he unrolled before me. On both sides of it were written words of lament and mourning and woe.

And he said to me, 'Son of man, eat what is before you, eat this scroll; then go and speak to the house of Israel.' So I opened my mouth, and he gave me the scroll to eat.

Then he said to me, 'Son of man, eat this scroll I am giving you and fill your stomach with it.' So I ate it, and it tasted as sweet as honey in my mouth.

He then said to me: 'Son of man, go now to the house of Israel and speak my words to them.'

Ezekiel 2:1—3:4

The word God asked Jeremiah and Ezekiel to deliver was a bitter warning of divine judgement. But Jeremiah testified that as he 'ate' God's words they were 'my joy and my heart's delight'. And Ezekiel, with similar reaction concerning the scroll he had ingested, said, 'It tasted as sweet as honey in my mouth.'

Similar terminology

Returning to John's account in Revelation 10, we find similar circumstances and terminology. God has a prophetic word for John to convey. It is a bitter word of impending divine judgement. As he ingests the word, it is honey sweet, but it turns his stomach sour.

Perhaps we have lost something in getting away from the old King James's 'bitter belly'—'As soon as I had eaten it, my belly was bitter.' There are 'happy-happy-happy' people in our churches who will insist that the word of God can never be anything but honey sweet. It is my contention, however, that the Christian believers who are intent upon being faithful witnesses for Jesus

Christ are not destined to always find sweetness and light in their contacts with evil, rebellious people.

When we digest, absorb, soak up the word of the Lord, it becomes part and parcel of our daily lives. It is our delight. It is honey and sweetness. But as we share that same word in our witness to lost men and women, we will know something of the bitterness and hostility— even enmity—that was the experience of John and Jeremiah and Ezekiel. There have been times when I have had to counsel believers who had become discouraged to the point of despair because of the treatment they had received at the hands of those who hated their witness.

There is another sense in which the word becomes bitterness within us. It becomes bitterness to our sinful nature, because the sinful nature 'desires what is contrary to the Spirit' (Galatians 5:17). There are people within our Christian fellowships who have determined to set their own agendas—to live their lives as they please. They expect to be recognised as Christians, but they will not bow to the controls God has built into His holy word and will. They read their Bibles—they even buy a new Bible every few years. They have enough spiritual knowledge to know that the commitment of their spirit, soul and body to the standards of God's word will mean some bitter house-cleaning within. But they have decided to take no step that will bring pain or sharpness or harshness into what is now for them a soft and easy profession of the Christian life.

These people are determined to manage the influence of the word of God in their lives rather than to allow the word of God to manage them day by day, hour by hour.

Not judgemental, but concerned

Some people have accused me of sitting in judgement. But I think I am examining, with Christian concern, the true spiritual condition of many within the church's ranks. There exists a mind-set within present-day Christianity that supposes no one should get into trouble or suffer embarrassment for Christ's sake.

What is our answer when the Holy Spirit whispers to us about the true nature of our professed love for Jesus Christ? Suppose a young man proclaims his love for a certain young woman and wants to have her for his wife. But there is a difficulty he must consider. The girl's father is hostile to the match, letting the young man know that if he shows up again, he may be invited to leave under threat of a baseball bat—or worse.

If that young man schemes of ways to see the girl regardless of her father's threats, I would call it a case of true love. But if he professes his love and then is frightened off by the threats, probably the girl was nothing more than a passing fancy.

I realise that my illustration has to do with human nature. Human nature is prone to measure the importance of benefits and to determine whether or not the benefits are worth the effort. Within our Christian setting, we presume we are talking about men and women who have been born again, brought out of darkness into light, transformed by the grace and mercy of God. They have tasted the benefits God has for them in Christ Jesus.

Throughout church history, millions of people have proven what it actually means to be loyal to Christ, what it means to say that Jesus Himself is more important than anything in this world.

'They tore at me!'

A number of years ago, in Chicago, I was in a car with several young people on our way to a youth rally. One of those in the car was a Jewish girl. Why she was with that Christian group I do not know, except that God's Spirit was still doing something in her life and soul. She told us of her experience in giving her heart to Jesus Christ and receiving Him as her Messiah. But afterwards, at home with her family and relatives, she encountered not only the traditional hatred for Jesus but actual physical abuse as well. I remember the chills I felt as she emotionally described how she was attacked.

'They tore at me! They screamed at me! They literally ripped my dress and clothes from my body and demanded that I repudiate my faith!'

'What did you do?' her young friends in the car asked.

I remember yet the anger in her answer. 'What could I do? It wasn't worth it! It wasn't worth what I had to put up with!' Yet, there she was, going with Christian friends to a youth rally. I never heard more about the girl. Deep in my heart, I believe that if she truly had found Jesus as her Messiah and Lord, God had something further for her. I do not think her angry outburst of 'It wasn't worth it' could have been the end of her faith.

I cannot describe what I feel deep within me when I hear of a Christian brother or sister who has suffered for the faith, or who has been martyred for the testimony of Jesus Christ. As I said earlier, my church is deeply involved in overseas missions. Just within the areas of my church's responsibility, it would be impossible to say how many faithful pastors and lay people have actually died for the faith. With a sense of distant admiration, we call them simple-hearted nationals. God calls them over-comers! Professing Christians in our North American churches can hardly comprehend so costly a price for the faith we take for granted. Material prosperity and popular acceptance have sapped the vitality of our witness.

It is a completely distorted view of true biblical faith to personify Christianity by the wealthy, back-slapping boisterous business person who measures success by bank accounts, big cars, palatial homes and expensive vacations. I certainly am not saying that successful and prosperous people cannot be Christians—the grace and mercy of God sees to that. My point is that Christianity, in so many instances, is being equated with material wealth and affluence. These are the conditions that are facing us in Christianity, not only in North America but in other nations as well.

Have we 'eaten the book'?

The question is this: What are we allowing the word of God to say to us, and what is our reaction to that word? Have we consumed and digested the book? Have we absorbed the word of God into our lives? Or are we among those content to be a part of a Christian congregation where there are no extreme demands, where fellowship will be consistently pleasant and without responsibility?

When we, as Christians, love our Lord Jesus Christ with heart and soul and mind, the word of God is on our side! If we could only grasp the fact that God's word is more than a book! It is the revelation of divine truth from the person of God Himself. It has come as a divine communication in the sacred Scriptures. It has come to us in the guidance and conviction imparted by the divine Spirit of God within our beings. It has been modelled for us in Jesus Christ, the incarnate Word and the eternal Son.

Probably the majority of people who have lived in this twentieth century have held and hold to the idea that God is silent. I have talked with people who supposed that God spoke the holy Scriptures into being and then lapsed into centuries-long silence.

God is *not* silent, and His love for His creation is such that He has never been silent. We should realise, for the good of our spiritual lives, that the Scriptures are effective in our beings because the Living Word is speaking in heaven and the Living Voice is sounding throughout the earth:

> This is love for God: to obey his commands. And his commands are not burdensome, for everyone born of God has overcome the world....
> And it is the Spirit who testifies, because the Spirit is the truth. For there are three that testify: the Spirit, the water and the blood; and the three are in agreement. We accept man's testimony, but God's testimony is greater because it is the testimony of God, which he has given about his Son. Anyone who believes in the Son of God has this testimony in his heart.
>
> *1 John 5:3–10*

We who preach the word of God do not have the facility for plain speech that the Holy Spirit imparted to John. Can words be more direct than these? 'This is love for God: to obey his commands.'

The act of committal to Jesus Christ in salvation releases us from the penalty of sin, but it does not release any of us from the obligation to obey the words of Christ, our Saviour. Rather, it brings us under the joyful necessity to obey. If we would have God's blessing upon us, we must begin to obey.

Mankind has not heeded God's word

In the Revelation we have noted again and again that God has been faithful in warning men and women that the end of this age will come and that the judgements of God will fall. In the vision given to John, it appears that the people of the last days had taken their own safety for granted. They were not disturbed about their future. Seemingly they ignored every indication that the God who created them was a person of His word. As a result, they were totally unprepared for death, judgement and eternity.

Conditions in our churches cause me to believe that many professing Christians are living under a similarly false sense of security. The Old Testament prophets consistently warned Israel about false security. Israel supposed that because the nation was especially chosen by God, everything else would fall into place. Messiah would come. They would hail Him. He would set up His rule on earth. All that they took for granted. But Messiah came, and they did not recognise Him. Their own religious leaders conspired to have Him crucified. How many in Israel had recognised Him? One in a thousand? One in ten thousand?

There are two kinds of tranquillity among us—not counting the tranquillisers a person can buy in bottles. There is the tranquillity that people find in just taking themselves and everything around them for granted. They tend to believe all kinds of good things about themselves—which are not really true. That is dangerous.

Then there is the true tranquillity that God has promised when the soul has been shaken to its foundation. There is little preaching about this kind of tranquillity in our day. Too often men and women get referred to psychiatrists rather than to God. If they would do what the Bible directs, they would take their disturbances and their alarms to God and to an open Bible. If the Holy Spirit is allowed to illuminate the word of God, the word will first do its surgery, but then it will mend what it has cut. The result is true tranquillity of soul, spirit and mind

They say it does not make sense

To the worldling this does not make sense. 'I will stick with the psychiatrist,' is his or her response. But the necessity for spiritual illumination before we can grasp spiritual truth is taught throughout the New Testament. God certainly has something to say to the seeking soul that He cannot impart to the person who ignores the truth and scorns the message in His word. Spiritual truths cannot be received in the ordinary ways of human nature.

When the Revelation warns against this world, it is not so much a warning against the ways of this world as it is against the spirit of this world. This present world, in the New Testament meaning of the word, is simply unregenerate human nature no matter where it is found, even in the midst of zealous devotion to religion.

When Jesus came into our midst and presented Himself as the Messiah, His greatest enemies were the entrenched religious leaders of Israel. Their spiritual principles were drawn not from above, but from below. They used all the tactics of unregenerate men, including bribes, to bring the witness of lies against Jesus. To defend God, they acted like the devil. To claim support from the Scriptures, they defied its true teachings. In the name of a religion of love and mercy, they loosed the reins of blind hate. So fierce was their spirit—the spirit of this world that dominated them—that it never rested until they had put to death the Son of God.

Now, we are evangelicals at a troubled time in history. We face a danger—the danger of taking for granted that because we are evangelicals in theology and creed, we are automatically pleasing in the sight of God. Is it possible that our conservative theology is really a kind of nibbling of God's sweet and precious word? Do we never allow it to become anything more than the creed and doctrines we say we believe?

The angel said to John, 'Eat the scroll! Consume it! Digest it!' Jeremiah and Ezekiel testified that they ate and digested the word of God, and then they went out to face bitterness and hostility. We are God's people for our day and our generation. God's people are called to be something different. God expects a certain kind of heroism from His redeemed people. Our call is not to a life of ease; we are called to be at our best for God and for His gospel.

The sweetness of the word stalls us

It appears at times that we are stalled by the sweetness of the word of God. What a dear and treasured gift it is! Maybe that is why we come to a halt. Maybe that is why we do not grow and mature in Christ as we should. We are being nurtured in the sweetness. We are prone, then, to refuse the discipline, to refuse the cross God lays upon us in the scoffing and ridicule of those who are still His enemies.

But Jesus is Victor! The faithful church in humility and submission will be exalted with Him, for ever and ever!

> Then I saw a new heaven and a new earth, for the first heaven and the first earth had passed away, and there was no longer any sea.... And I heard a loud voice from the throne saying, 'Now the dwelling of God is with men, and he will live with them. They will be his people, and God himself will be with them and be their God....'
>
> He who was seated on the throne said, 'I am making everything new!' Then he said, 'Write this down, for these words are trustworthy and true.'...
>
> I did not see a temple in the city, because the Lord God Almighty and the Lamb are its temple. The city does not need the sun or the moon to shine on it, for the glory of God gives it light, and the Lamb is its lamp. The nations will walk by its light, and the kings of the earth will bring their splendour into it. On no day will its gates ever be shut, for there will be no night there. The glory and honour of the nations will be brought into it. Nothing impure will ever enter it, nor will anyone who does what is shameful or deceitful, but only those whose names are written in the Lamb's book of life.
>
> *Rev 21:1,3,5,22–27*

On that day, the whole earth and all creation shall know it: Jesus Christ is Victor! Amen!

The Knowledge of the Holy

by A. W. Tozer

'The church has surrendered her once lofty
concept of God and has substituted for it one so
low, so ignoble, as to be utterly unworthy of
thinking, worshipping men. With our loss of a
sense of majesty has come the further loss of
religious awe and sense of the divine presence.
We have lost our spirit of worship and our
ability to withdraw inwardly to meet God in
adoring silence.'
(from the Author's Introduction)

Dr Tozer encourages us to understand the
character of God and rediscover His majesty in a
way that will deeply affect our day-to-day living.

A. W. Tozer

 *STL Books*

The Pursuit of God

by A. W. Tozer

'This book is a modest attempt to aid God's hungry children so to find Him. Nothing here is new except in the sense that it is a discovery which my own heart has made of spiritual realities most delightful and wonderful to me. Others before me have gone much farther into these holy mysteries than I have done, but if my fire is not large it is yet real, and there may be those who can light their candle at its flame.'

(from the author's Preface)

STL Books

Men Who Met God

by A. W. Tozer

For men and women who have met God, we may say that the sun—the Son—has come up in their hearts and His warmth and light have given them a distinguishing radiance.

First, these great souls always have a compelling sense of God Himself. Second, it it plain that the significance of their personal experiences remains sharp and clear. The third element is the permanent and life-changing nature of a true encounter with God.

A. W. Tozer

In *Men Who Met God*, Tozer looks at seven Old Testament saints—Abraham, Isaac, Jacob, Moses, Elijah, Isaiah and Ezekiel. Each of these men had life-changing encounters with God. From their lives, lived in the ancient Middle East, Tozer finds application to men and women of today.

STL Books

The Root of the Righteous

by A. W. Tozer

A. W. Tozer lamented the fact that many of his contemporaries were concerned only with the fruit of their faith rather than the root.

'Much that passes for Christianity today,' he observed, 'is the brief bright effort of the severed branch to bring forth its fruit in its season. Immediate "results" are all that matter, quick proofs of present success without a thought of next week or next year.'

Tozer reminds us that the fruit of our Christian lives demands patient waiting, and urges us to ensure that we are rooted and built up in Christ.

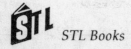

STL Books